TRUMPING A FIXED DECK

Defying Insurmountable Odds and (All) Statistics Resoundingly

By

Haneef Sabree

TRUMPING A FIXED DECK

Defying Insurmountable Odds and (All) Statistics Resoundingly

Copyright© 2011   by Haneef Sabree

All rights reserved. No part of this book may be reproduced, stored in a retrieval system, or transmitted by any means without the expressed written permission of the author.

First printing: 2012

Cover design: Daniel Harrison Jr.—The greatest artist I have ever known.

Co-Editor: Yvelette Stines

Graphic Designer: Patricia Rasch

Back cover photograph: Courtesy of Timothy Paule

Published by Young Breed Publications, Inkster, MI 48141

Email: hjsabree@att.net

Website: jrhandsonsllc.dudaone.com

Library of Congress Catalog Card Number: 2012930768

ISBN: 978-0-9846633-1-6 (pbk.)

The Paradox of Our Time

The paradox of our time in history is that we have taller buildings, but shorter tempers; wider freeways, but narrower viewpoints; we spend more, but have less; we buy more, but enjoy it less.

We have bigger houses and smaller families; more conveniences, but less time; we have more degrees, but less sense; more knowledge, but less judgment; more experts, but more problems; more medicine, but less wellness.

We drink too much, smoke too much, spend too recklessly, laugh too little, drive too fast, get angry too quickly, stay up too late, get up too tired, read too seldom, watch TV too much, and pray too seldom.

We have multiplied our possessions, but reduced our values. We talk too much, love too seldom, and hate too often. We've learned how to make a living, but not a life; we've added years to life, not life to years.

We've been all the way to the moon and back, but have trouble crossing the street to meet the new neighbor. We've conquered outer space, but not inner space; we've done larger things, but not better things.

We've cleaned up the air, but polluted the soul; we've split the atom, but not our prejudice.

We write more, but learn less; we plan more, but accomplish less. We've learned to rush, but not to wait; we have higher incomes, but lower morals; we have more food, but less appeasement; we build more computers to hold more information to produce more copies than ever, but have less communication; we've become long on quantity, but short on quality.

These are the times of fast foods and slow digestion; tall men, and short character; steep profits, and shallow relationships. These are the times of world peace, but domestic warfare; more leisure, but less fun; more kinds of food, but less nutrition.

These are days of two incomes, but more divorce; of fancier houses, but broken homes. These are days of quick trips, disposable diapers, throw away morality, one-night stands, overweight bodies, and pills that do everything from cheer to quiet to kill.

It is a time when there is much in the show window and nothing in the stockroom.

~Dalai Lama

Dedicated to the community of Inkster, Michigan
& all those whose voices are never heard.

Table of Contents

KIPUPWE xi
JRH AND SONS LLC HISTORY xiii

POETRY

1 Reason 2 Smile 3
Cooly D 4
2TheLaastfrmtheFstBorne 5
A Poor Man's Riches 6
Bludlynes 7
Ain't to be Faded 8
Armed & Ready 9
Because U R a Nigger 10
Black Prints 13
Bac Against Da Wall 14
Crucial Contemplations 15
Cryin' N Da Streetz 16
Death is Closer than My Shadow 17
Dablakkisteyei 18
Winter Breeze 19
A Woman Defined, 3 of a Kind 20
Edutamemeant 21
The Girl I Neva Nu 23
Forget Me Not 24
Fatal Reflections 25

Gone But Not Forgotten	26
Instead of Tears	27
I Didn't Know	28
If I Go	30
Implosions 2 the Psyche	31
Inktown	32
Nightmare Not On Elm Street	33
Intercessions	34
It Ain't Easy Being Me	35
The Sweetest Woman I Eva Knew	36
Hopeful Currents	37
More Than a Girlfriend	38
Most High, I Tried	39
My Wife to Be	40
My Dead Homies	42
Neva Breached	43
Never On My Knees	44
GughD Niitte	45
Family Photographs	46
No Mean Muggs	50
No Time 2 Say Good Bye	51
Photo Finish	52
Oblivious 2 Change	53
Good Guy Gott Got	54
Unbrakdounabowl	56
No Matter the Cost	57
Undeniable Truth	58
Can't Let It Rydd	59
Neva My Fate	61

Humble Got Shot	62
Tru Retrospect	63
I Thought We Was Cool	64
The Cards I was Dealt	65
Alltahm	66
President 4 the People	67
Rainbow Lynn	68
Respect Affiliated	69
Role Modelz	70
Shine Again	71
Shortie Got Style	72
The Dream and I	73
Tiger Claw	74
Playin' Against a Fixed Deck	75
Souljas Can You Hear Me	76
K 2 Da' A	77
The Young Lady Off Brooklane	78
Words of a Soulja	79
Who Am I?	80
Wonda Woman	81
Where Ever U R	82
Ruptured Heart	83
Ever Ask Why	84
Ladi Chi	86
Put Your Fists ↑	87
Black Rage	89
Acec of Spadez	90
Bonus Trac	91
Frozen in Time	92

SHORT STORIES

The Journey Within.. 94
The True Man of Steel 99
Proposal.. 103

PARTING THOUGHTS

Kiangazi.. 108
Elimu 109
Noda 111
Imani 112
Afya 113
Kutaalamika 115
~Ventricular Soliloquies~ 123
Special Thanks.. 124
Remembered Eternal 125
The Only Way to Win 126

KIPUPWE

In life, one can never change the past, so it's important that we all try to live for today and tomorrow. In decision making, it's imperative that you think for yourself, evaluate, observe and analyze any situation you encounter before you make impactful decisions. Understand that you are the pilot of your own plane, but the nature of your destination is dependent upon your preparedness and state of mind.

In the process of planning/goal setting, you owe it to yourself to set high expectations, nothing less will do. As commanders (future leaders) of the nation you have all the tools that the most renowned men and women ever had: two arms, two legs, and a brilliant mind when you choose to use it in an effective and positive way.

Investigate and learn about yourself to realize that just because something or someone is good to you, it doesn't mean they are best for you. Take ample time to learn about your history, such as the marvelous civilizations of Ghana, Mali, and Timbuktu. If you fail to do this, you won't have sufficient knowledge of the whole self, without this comprehensive knowledge it would be difficult to truly love yourself, and you will be like a garden without fertile soil. Within our communities and culture, we need real trailblazers, men and women, to step up to the plate. Far too many brothers and sisters have already sold out their communities and turned their backs on the people.

Keep in mind, we are all connected and one with the people, not above the people. We must learn to love our sisters, brothers, and family because in the end that's all we have. Strive to carry out each day as though it will be your last. We owe it to the ancestors, who gave their life so we could have a better tomorrow, those who care about us and most importantly ourselves. There are three particulars promised to you in this world/life: the righteous will prevail over the wicked, the truth will triumph over the lie, and with hope integrated in faith nothing is impossible or unattainable.

* A Penny 4 Your Thoughts *

"He who is not courageous enough to take risks will accomplish nothing in life." –Muhammad Ali

"One must learn to walk before they can fly, you cannot fly into flight." -Unknown

"A man/woman who pays respect to the great paves the way for his own greatness." –African Proverb (Things Fall Apart)

"The journey of a thousand miles begins with a single step."—Confucius

"Education is our passport to the future, for tomorrow belongs to the people who prepare for it today." –Malcolm X

"When an elder dies a library burns." –African Proverb

"When there is no enemy within, the enemies outside cannot hurt you." –African Proverb

JRH AND SONS LLC HISTORY

*I*nitially registered on June 26, 1980 by Dennis Sabree, JRH AND SONS is the offspring of PHERC Corporation. PHERC was Plumbing, Heating, Electrical, and Refrigeration Mechanical Company, founded by our beloved late grandpa—John Raleigh Harrison Senior. Our limited liability company's initials are a humble tribute to his progressive professional life.

JRH AND SONS LLC's mission statement is to make affordable housing in developing neighborhoods available to young, married, and working couples living in Southeast Michigan. Although, young, married, working couples have been targeted as the desired recipients of nicely renovated homes, other qualified applicants will be given equal consideration.

Through blood, sweat, and tears the foundation began here:
The original members of JRH & SONS –from left to right:
John Raleigh Harrison (grandfather), Dion Van Irvin (uncle),
Daniel Harrison (uncle), and Dennis Sabree (father)

POETRY

Dedicated 2: Asha ☺

1 Reason 2 Smile

This place can get incredibly stressed
From above I seek calm & rest
Don't know how results became such a mess
Her spirit provides a mental vest
In her I found a reason 2 smile

Her aura is more resplendent
Than one thousand regal doves
She had to be sent from the abundant
Gardens far above

When the reaper takes my life
The Lil' Angel I will always luv
When the world tries 2 play me 4 a scrub
All I need is her strengthening hug
In her I found a reason 2 smile

Too often people ignore my shouts
Pockets on thin don't have much clout
I know this isn't what life is about

When my mind is racing with endless doubt
Witnessing my souljas succumbin' 2 an obvious rout
Innumerable days I feel there's no way out
In her I found a reason 2 smile

Cooly D

2TheLaastfrmtheFstBorne

Accountability is copious,
U kicked off the circle of life,
All u can do (in this world) is try,
Non-receptive to the ravenous,
Negative advice,
They look up 2 u,
So naturally,
Synthesize wise choices,
& do the best u can do,
When u hone in your mind 2 it,
U will have annexed,
The "Sword of Thundera" view,
Your uncle is mightily proud,
Of the young women and men,
U have transcended in 2.

A Poor Man's Riches

Worth more than platinum and gold,
Yet so precious to life,
Greater than the seven wonders of the world,
Deeper than any ocean filled with pearls,
Far exceeding any material,
Genuine,
Truly magnificent.

Bludlynes

I know a gang of "Joes" who
tried to hang me with a rope.

The system flooded the Black communities
with guns, alcohol, propaganda, and dope.

Far too many people have given up on hope
but I'll never let my mind go broke.

My visions break the limits of the world's best telescopes
you can save all that fakeness & bullsh$t for the Roman Pope.

My soldiers are hard to hit like a molecule of transparent smoke
all you Uncle Toms and crooked bureaucrats will be dealt slit throats.

Numerous days on this earth a brother can't cope
but relentlessly I'm inflicting mental murder and devastation to all you jokes.

Annihilating the plagues of my Black folks
by servin' them that scantless antidote.

TRUMPING A FIXED DECK

Ain't to be Faded

Nice brothas often finish last
Why fools test me I must ask
If you play me there won't be a 2nd chance
I'll be there, my doggz, for the last dance
Back-biters & snakes flood my every glance
It's the ones you think are close that sometimes
leave you flat on you're a$#
Keepin' it real is the only way I know,
The days are numbered for all my foes.
Scads of busters try to clown my city
So there's no way I can show them pity
You respect me & I'll respect you
It doesn't matter if your (skin) color is blue
Until the day I die I'll always stay true
Betrayal is like having your insides ripped out
But I'm a soulja no doubt
I will take my losses
While I blow the whole scene out
Holding it down from the north to the south
Stay out my grill cause your best bet is to
close your mouth.

Representin': The Meadowlane Boyz (Ben, Rashard, Vincent, Degaryen, Ontario, Kwan, A.D., Stanley and Sheldon Stegall), Wen, AO, Smok, Levi, Alex, Sweetz—The Shareefs, Khalid—The Muhammads, D-Bird, Ced, Corey, KG, Kyle, Jason, Jamar, P-Loc, DeMario, N.A. Rasheed, Eugene, Dion, M. Rashad, Chris, Pone, Dante, B-Hawk, Misty & all my comrades puttin' it down

Armed & Ready

In order 2 competitively battle
U have 2 have a team
The days of the "Lone Ranger" r nothin' but a dream
Rain, sleet, or snow
Since the days of old
My compadres are ready 2 go
Toe to toe
Blow 4 blow
Flow 4 flow
It'll b wise 4 u 2 act like u know
Thru the catastrophes
They bounce back instinctively
Wielding that hammer
Crushin' all archenemies
Don't misapprehend peaceful
With a state of passivity
My rydaz stay armed n arsenal
2 the umph degree
We are acute & connected
Parallelin'
The bonds n chemistry.

Because U R a Nigger

The "Fab Five" brought in millions of dollars to the University of Michigan
More than quadrupled the revenue from the sales of U of M sports paraphernalia
In comparison 2 previous years they boosted the schools overall prestige
How could the university take down the banners they earned?
And try 2 erase them from the history books?
Why did the Michigan alumni refer to the Fab Five As coons & criminals?
Because they're niggers.

Why is it so hard to buy a house?
All of the necessary requirements were in place
Performance was above and beyond with the utmost professionalism
Yet they still made sure the deal didn't close
Cause u a nigger.

When I'm with my woman
Sometimes trick a$# brothas
But mainly potato chip a#% immigrants
and Caucasian males try 2 belittle me
Until I put that nine with hollows 2 the chin
Now they want 2 B Mr. Friend
That sh$# is worse than sin
Fu#$ a grin
It's because u r a nigger.

When I go 2 varying places of business
The employees particularly give me strange looks
And their attitudes are so flagitious
That ain't right!
I feel u lil' soulja
It's because u r a nigger.

At the Ambassador Bridge Customs stop
It's appalling 2 hear about the uncivilized behavior of
Officer keebler, dikes' & low-lifes' 1-2-3 wrongly detaining the 2 of u
Grossly violating your rights
& writing u off as an average dope peddler from the Porter blocc
They viewed us as some niggers.

How could they call the victims of Hurricane Katrina refugees?
Leaving a manifold of souls lorn & dispossessed
Then turn around & allow rich white capitalists 2 buy up the land that
Blacks once owned and/or lived on
Cause they r niggers.
And…
The barbarity, execution of Troy Davis
Seven out of nine witnesses recanted their original statements
Overwhelming doubt was magnanimous
The supposed murder weapon was never linked to the accused
His plea for a new trial was still denied
A prime substantiation of the failure, heinousness of capital punishment
Coalesced with a fatally flawed judicial system
They considered my brotha a nigger.

It's shameful how the 1st Lady and current President are verbally attacked
Disrespected, and subjected 2 unjustifiable criticism
Perpetrators especially from the Tea Party
Have committed untold acts of treason with no repercussions
Previous presidents are the central reason why America was headed 4 total destruction
No president has had 2 deal with the over-the-top foolishness and shenanigans

TRUMPING A FIXED DECK

From the (3) public, (1) politicians, and (2) cretinous television hosts
Consonant 2 the 44th elect
I think I can conceptualize where u r coming from now.

Am I a nigger uncle?
"Hell no!"
Don't u eva think that,
But u r my *N.I.G.G.A
U r adorned with tuition and a rare set of skillz
That makes u more powerful than any heartless trigger
The truth and divine order
Will expose who's the actual niggers.

*Never Ignorant Getting Goals Accomplished
(1) Michael Steele, Sarah Palin, Joe Wilson, etc.
(2) Bill O'Reilly, Glynn Beck, etc.
(3) Donald Trump, citizens, etc.

Black Prints

Each new day
Is a chance anew
Rainbow lit skies
Perfect my view

Teach the children
So that their roots are strong
Make them understand
Being Black is nothin' wrong

Quite frankly it's wonderful
And should be carried with a smile
Their history is so rich
Extraordinarily profound

Never believe our ancestry started as mere
Slaves, jesters, & clowns
Sistas, brothas always embrace your brown skin
Cause the greatest love of all starts from within

This world would be nothing without the influence of blacks
It's not my opinion
4 if you look deep into history
You'll see it's an actual fact
Can you do 4 me this 1 favor?
Teach the lil' souljas the world is their map.

Bac Against Da Wall

I'm drownin' in deep H2O
But I refuse to die.

Most of my old public school teachers
Told me nothin' but lies.

I'm dodging shots to the dome
When I try to reach the masses.
There's nobody home.

The bustas invoke my retaliation
I'll leave them all with permanent mutilations
 Narrow-minded fools could never grasp my wicked compilations.

The H2O is way over my head
 But I'm still not dead.

If me and my people don't get some freedom
There will be bloodshed.

Crucial Contemplations

As I stroll through the earth,
I've witnessed the value of life,
See unlike a video game you can't die twice,
It's easy to blame the white man for all the strife,
But too often when I turn my back,
It's my own people with the knife,
So as you see the root of the problem is spliced,
Being too nice in life will never suffice,
Knowing the core of the problem is half the fight,
So encapsulate the finer things of life,
Be on guard as if it's your last night,
Cause you only have 1 life.

Cryin' N Da Streetz

Yeah youngsters str8 shootin' n da streetz
Hell yeah
They got beef
When they were young
U mutherfu$#?% left them 4 their lonesome
Bleedin' viscerously
So steep
Cryin' n da streetz
4 all 2 c.

Death is Closer than My Shadow

I've already had close encounters with death
How much longer before I take 2 to da' chest
Dudes nowadays for nothin'
Will leave u with a hole n da neck
I had plenty of reality checks
This life man
Is so complex
History has proven
Souljas with my beliefs
Become early partners with the grips of death
I never expected to live a long sum
Cause 2 often the good do fade away young
But dam%
I was tryin' to have a couple daughters
Two maybe three sons
However the "wolf blades"
And treacherous "gunz"
Got a brothas heart & soul stung
It's only a question of when
Before I'm the 1
I try 2 summarize what I've done
The relentless external + internal clashes
frequently make it ineffable 2 have fun
whether I'm dead or breathin'
a new day will have begun

Dablakkisteyei

I am what I am
I wouldn't have it any other way
You may not feel what I say
But you better be at least twice as good
If some day
You plan to parlay
With all the traps and tricknology
Why is it hard to understand
The reasons so many go astray

Public figures sell me lies
While they hold my plight at bay
I'm telling you man
It's a rigged game
That I'm forced to play
If you choose not to abide by the fox's rules and obey
On the concrete you're liable to lay

Sometimes I feel like a living dream
As pieces to my puzzle straight fade away
Undeterred by it all
I'm thankful for every day

Can't forget the kings & queens
Who went through havoc to carve a gateway
Call me a heat sinker
Cause I'm locked on victory's prey
And if your sums don't equal my 1's
Just flash back to when I begun
Because you won't feel what I say

Winter Breeze

TRUMPING A FIXED DECK

DEDICATED TO: CHRISTINA,
LESLIE AND RHONDA

A WOMAN DEFINED, 3 OF A KIND

FROM CHRISTINA, RHONDA 2 LESLIE,
BACK 2 THE DAYS OF MEEK ELEMENTARY,
I OBSERVED SOME GRAND TAPESTRY,
THE PERFECT EXAMPLE OF WHAT A WOMAN
IS SUPPOSE 2 B,
MY SISTERS DEFINE IT WITH CLARITY,
LIFE LESSONS LEARNED BECAME RUDIMENTARY,
UNTIL I'M NO LONGER BREATHING,
I WILL LOVE THEM UNCONDITIONALLY,
THEY ARE A BLESSING U C,
ESSENTIAL N DEVELOPING,
THE WARRIOR N NEEF.

Edutamemeant

Removing discipline from the schools?
So much 4 relying on intellectuals,
Those who r chargeable,
R niggardly educated loons,
The high siddities,
Implanted virulent seeds which in turn,
Harvest students who presently confront teachers,
In addition 2,
Brandishing a disdain 4 basic rules,
God has no place,
Inside our primary & secondary institutes,
But everything else is admissible,
Now kids are shootin' up lecture rooms,
Don't worry about thinkin' for yourself,
We will guarantee that u r trained,
When u graduate,
No need 2 b autonomous,
U can insure our establishment is maintained,
We'll spoon-feed u The Dibels, Everyday Math, and The 6 + 1
Writing Traits,
Directly into your cerebral membrane,
If u have an active upper story and struggle in mathematics,
We won't stimulate your confidence,
I'll diagnose u with ADHD and Dyscalculia,
Chronologically ship u 2,
The physician (PCP) & special ed instructor,
They will then have to deal wit u,
Despite the fact these fundamentals bestow upon u the quintessential
Contrivances 2 navigate thru life,
Developing Life Skills aren't esteemed,

TRUMPING A FIXED DECK

Just concentrate on achieving As or Bs,
& makin' the Dean,
Any academician who goes against the grain,
Don't fret children & cowardly conniving colleagues,
Their teaching career,
Will be found slain,
The parents are kept mis-educated,
Uninvolved,
And uninformed,
So they can stringently swoop down and unconscionably harass,
Cogent teachers as Desert Storm,
First-rate educators,
Produce lawyers, surgeons, and masterminds,
Who design technological airplanes,
 4 compensation,
Preceptors r apportioned at the derrière of the economic chain,
Abject administrators will continue to procure padded salaries,
Albeit to leadership abilities & standards,
Flaccid,
Tantamount 2 a stalk of flaky,
Decadent celery.

The Girl I Neva Nu

She seemed so refined,
Like a ray from the sun,
When I first saw her I knew she was the one,
The physique & beauty she possessed,
Was clearly unmatched by the rest,
She had hidden treasures inside,
That she failed 2 realize,
Thou she was as pretty as a rose,
The potential she withheld,
Appeared quite froze,
I thought the situation between us,
Was cooler than a breeze,
But the fact remains,
She's the sweet sugar,
I never even began 2 have.

Forget Me Not

In hustling to reach the top I fall
Forget me not

While tryin' to uplift my comrades & the babies
Cause they're hurtin'
I may get stalled
Forget me not

In exposing the truths of this hypocritical world
To cement the base fo' my lil' future boys and girls
If only I could live carefree as a Belle Isle squirrel
There's a chance I may be taken for that final whirl
Forget me not

When my life surpasses low
Perhaps by hands of my own
Forgive them
For they did that which they didn't know
The origins of that
Date back
To slavery, Willie Lynch, tricknology, and dough

That's why our unity, self-worth and morale
is so crippling slow
I ain't tryin' to hear that though

The light
Regardless 1 day will show
If I get got
Or cease to flow
1-luv to all those who are close, ghost, in jail, and po'
Forget me not.

Fatal Reflections

Every time I reflect
It makes me want to grab the tec
I'm hearing voices in my head
All these people are walking around dead
My moms and pops get the ultimate props
Without the two my life would've already stopped
They sacrificed so much so a brother could grow
There's no way in hell I'm going out like a h$
If I die early in the game
Please don't shed too many tears
Stay strong in the struggle there's no room for fear
Don't get me wrong I'm not ready to leave
All I'm saying is there's no need to grieve
I can't forget my sisters & brother and all my no limit soldiers
They've been by my side like Bonnie & Clyde
For all you envious fake bustas: senators, lobbyists, prison guards the whole f$#king slew
All you other sucka-a$# politicians, benedicts, and po-pos are included too
I got a whole bunch of slugs and they're just for you
I realize in this world brains prevail over brawn
But the fire in my eyez burns brighter than Spawn
As I constantly keep hittin' the deck
It makes me want to grab for the tec

TRUMPING A FIXED DECK

Dedicated to: Tupac Amaru Shakur

Gone But Not Forgotten

Foreshadowed by brotha Malcolm, G. Jackson & F. Hampton
Courtesy of the Bureau
They assassinated my hero

Claimed it was a random hit
Ain't that some sh#t
Showcased gross negligence & a disregard for procedures

With no concern for the culprits,
The case has implications of law enforcement
Officials involvement written all over it

Resulting in the scene being condensed & clouded
He motivated & spear-headed programs for the youth
Disseminated knowledge and exposed the truth

U had 2 feel
That fire, soul and the real
As he integrated charisma and flair
But it was that delivery

In which u could not compare
Utterances directly touched
Those whose sentiments are
Usually overlooked or abused

Those pantaloons got the game confused
I'm going to bump your music til' I die
Because that's how souljas do

Instead of Tears

What I thought was compassion & love,
In actuality formulated hurt and pain,
Through life lessons and realizations,
I have learned 2 breathe once again,
The shackles of sorrow and misery,
Escorted by emotional & psychological strain,
Have been released 4ever from my heart,
Replaced with genuine change,
I now know unequivocally,
What finally set me free,
The fact that I begin loving me.
Thus capturing the state of happiness,
Which was the agenda,
From the start,
Progressing undauntedly forward,
Instead of tears,
Light has extinguished the dark.

I Didn't Know

I ain't never had much,
My blood made sure,
I had enough,
Dem' streetz is so ruff,
Life is no bluff,
You have to be tuff,
Listen and keep your mouth shut,
There you go spittin' again,
Are you an unloaded clip?,
Reapin' the bling of this life,
Without putting n the sacrifice,
School is in session,
Only 4 periods to go,
The title of the classes are,
Pimp, hustla, gangsta, & h$,
Can't tell ya nathin',
Cause you already know,
Forgot to tell you about,
The crooked po-po,
What about the devastation,
Of having no role model(s),
And the impact of a slug from a heartless .44,
Shady trick a$# niggas stealin' your dough,
Or that white negro aka city council,
Where's the monie 4 the baby bottle,
What u know about the scantless hizz&$ who constantly lure,
And the helluva deathtrap,
The corner liquor store,
Folks on they knees cryin' 2 the Lord,
Yet still you slang & use that dope even more,

Havin' 2 choose between slangin' or survival,
Is a bit#$ 2 da' core,
What if when the uzi sprays your lil' niece don't make it to the floor,
Dam&!
So now the feds are at the door,
Stuck with 3 meals and a cot,
Your cradle got rocked,
Shanked cause you got caught up in a plot,
Never really had a fair shot,
Left 6 feet deep to rot,
Wishin' you had another chance,
To "lite" up the spot,
Reduced to a memory,
Knowin' few will remember me,
Smoked like a blunt,
Cause I didn't know.

If I Go

If I don't make it to 50,
At least know I tried to give plenty,
It's a da%n shame thou,
The way they murdered my homie Moe,
Instead of pouring out some liquor,
I'll pay homage to him bigga,
By erecting in memory of his name,
A monumental center,
I need to do more dhikr,
Cause the pain is gettin' steeper,
I wanted a wife and some kids,
I put that on everything I did,
But what I want is not how it always is,
I reflect on the days at the sand lot,
Nowadays guns & glocks go pop,
Resolutions and answers I search 4 n thoughts,
If I go,
Forget me not,
Cause faith, perseverance, & madd heart, is what we got,
And It'll never stop,
Not even when that casket drops.

Implosions 2 the Psyche

Flashes of gluttony,
Can lead to a lifetime terminally inflamed,
Educate yourself about the realities of sensuality & sexuality,
Before being showered with acid hellish rain,
Otherwise,
Become an unwelcomed guess,
& take that long walk,
To the hospital room,
As u await to hear from the doctor,
Your uninvited doom,
Implosions 2 the psyche!
A C-4 boom,
If u let it overtake u,
That could be the omega,
I presume,
Contrary to that fatal cerebral split,
Don't u ever forget,
Only God knows the intentions,
In a man or woman's heart,
Climatically,
It's not how you start in this world,
It's how you finish the tune
Not how you start in this world,
How you finish that tune.

Inktown

Instills the cold facts of life,
Made up of the true & phony,
A place to just chill and kick it with your homies,
There are those who strive hard to make a decent buck,
Whereas others get caught slippin' and are out of luck,
Despite all the slander surrounding the city,
You can own businesses or flourish with a monopoly,
You can be your own man or lady,
Without having to smile in someone's face who you know is shady,
Much love to all the sisters who respect their precious selves,
In a town filled with the best of soldiers and my peoples' who are down
For whatever,
A place to sit back and think or lounge to the fullest,
To all those who know the real deal,
Forget you haters,
There is no place like Inktown.

Dedicated to: Sallie Mae & Nelneta

Nightmare Not On Elm Street

She said she loved me and wanted 2 b with me 4ever,
But that was just a lie,
I wish I would have known 4eva meant six months,
Quite short of the summer in July,
No barbeques,
Or walks in the park,
Nor conversations on the Detroit River b4 dark,
I gave her kindness & love,
As a reward she wiped her feet on my heart,
They say Hell knows no fury like a woman scorned,
That first hand I dearly learned,
The more love and compassion toward her I turned,
Her vengeance was sure 2 storm,
And she unleashed words,
That cut worse than the best double-edge swords,
But I just couldn't let go,
Because I loved her inconceivably so,
The damage done,
Did she ever really love me?
Only the Creator & her heart shall truly know.

Intercessions

Thoughts run rampant in my head,
Too many cats are overly fed,
Brothas are blind with 20/20 vision,
Can't you see whose causing the division,
Splitting us into pieces like a centrifuged atom,
Shortcuts are quick,
But a legacy is forever,
Wakeup my souljas,
Cause I can't conceive failure,
They plot on my life,
Every got da%n day,
Conspiring up ways,
To tap computer chips in my brainwaves,
But those cowards will never take my pride,
Not even if this brotha weren't alive,
So keep shootin' fo' the gates,
And fine tune that masterpiece called the mind,
For our ancestors were far ahead of their time,
Even though American History planted seeds,
Sprouting 1 of the deadliest forms of mental pollution around,
The lie.

It Ain't Easy Being Me

Every day that I wake
I see life is hell for a brotha.
They want me in a pen
as the gov't tries to do me in.
I'll keep holdin' on tho'
for there's no time to fold.
I have to represent for all sistas and brothas
left hangin' thin.
Many didn't make it
now their one with the wind.
I'm a man no doubt
but I can't lie cause it hurts.
As I stand tall against it all
I see life is hell for a brotha
And it ain't easy being me.

TRUMPING A FIXED DECK

DEDICATED TO: MAMA

THE SWEETEST WOMAN I EVA KNEW

I COULD NEVER PAINT A MORE PERFECT PICTURE,
OR IMAGINE MY LIFE WITHOUT HER TENDER,
FROM DAY 1 THROUGH HER I KNEW I WAS A WINNER,
COULD NEVER FORGET ALL THE SOULFUL HOT DINNERS,
THE HUGS, KISSES & HOW SHE REMOVED WOOD SPLINTERS,
INSTRUMENTAL IN ELEVATIN' ME FROM A BEGINNER,
GROOMED ME WITH SKILLS 2 B THE #1 CONTENDER,
NEVER A PRETENDER,
A NO QUITTER,
MOTIVATION & CHARACTER BUILDER,
A STR8 QUEEN DESCENDER,
I WISH I COULD DIE B4 HER & MY FATHER,
THAT'S (QUITE) SELFISH,
BUT I DO,
NOTHIN' IS MORE ABSOLUTELY TRUE,
2 MY MAMA DEAREST,
MOST SINCERELY,
THE SWEETEST WOMAN I EVA KNEW,
IS U.

Hopeful Currents

More Than a Girlfriend

When my baby said 4ever,
It was real,
Never concerned with her turning on me,
Or facilitating perfidy,
My gyrl was the deal,
Khaleelah was sassy,
Set her off,
& that attitude could get extremely nasty,
Get her heated,
Compositional status,
Left riddled & depleted,
If provoked,
Leelah discharged unimaginable pain,
Endanger her man,
Result is a twisted frame,
Had my back so tough,
U would have inferred she was deranged,
The luv babygyrl held down 4 me,
Was the antonym 2 mundane,
What happen next,
Is so strange,
1 day,
She came up missin',
2 this day,
I'm still trippin',
Because she was the best I eva had,
Much more than a girlfriend

Most High, I Tried

Before I die,
I wanted to let you know I tried,
I intended to do what was right,
Hard times, despair, temptation & trials n life,
Was cuttin' like a butcher knife,
When it came 2 Black women,
I feel I failed more than twice,
I tried treatin' them real nice,
It seems 4 that I paid the ultimate price,
But I won't complain about da piece I was sliced,
I strived to be positive and an example 4 the youth,
Cause the ones who were suppose to lead,
Dismissed them & said there's no use,
I tried to represent the truth,
Keepin' my character full proof,
I always give complete credit & respect 2 U,
Society is so "threw,"
My black people keep getting' stepped on too,
Makes me wanna blow off more than the roof,
1-luv to my blood and the real ones who,
The divine breath of life was blew,
Optimism will always hold true,
B4 the homie dies,
I just wanted to let you know,
Most High,
I did try

My Wife to Be

My wife to be,
It's a trip how she left me,
Just me, myself, alone,
I have to move on,
She ain't never comin' home,
Where has all the time gone,

I won't blame myself for all the wrong,
No doubt she had it going on,
I kept the lovin' strong,
Fully devoted to the bond stayin' prolonged,
It wasn't enough to keep the relationship sound,

Religion misunderstood,
Produces a deadly,
Divisive compound,
I must say a deadly destructive compound,
Some of her parasitic family & friends,
Especially church members & the reverend,
Insured that we became unwound,

While I wasn't around,
Her heart grew fonder,
For a trick in town,
On da real,
Some scandalous betrayal sh#% I found,
Comparable to Samson and Dhalila once expound,

I have stealthy eyez,
But the facts & red flags I failed to see,

I just knew she was the 1 for me,
Come 2 find out,
Princess E was trickin' on me,

4 how long is a mystery,
I sacrificed it all for thee,
Gave her my utmost intensity,
Greater than the limits of insanity,
In return she back-stabbed me,
How can this be?

For certain she was the woman to extend my family tree,
Instead she left a soulja with nothin' but anguish & grief,
Memories that can't repeat,
"Threes" I'm still hittin',
4 betta days,
I'm reminiscin'.

My Dead Homies

I contemplate endless times
On why my generals had to die
The pain gets hella vicious
When I try to analyze
In this life many soldiers seem to
Vanish way before their time
I can't sit in a corner and cry though
I'll leave that for the bit$%&#
Before I'm pushin' up daisies
I refuse to crack or go crazy
I'll leave a blaze on all you bit$%&#
For my dead homies.

Neva Breached

A sundry of trials
numberless raised eye brows
I just don't know
Steadily warding off
The most damagin' blow
No 1 has the time
Too occupied
Or on the go Plus the monies low
No where 2 turn
& the losses
R taking their toll
Feelin' the lash
From societies horror show
Intrinsically
Faithfully
In the steps of my ancestry
With perfection as in the laws of astrology
My spirit is energized
Within me
So though physically
due 2 the constant cancers of society
my body may be weak
but my soul still speaks
mind is free
because I'm n sync
with the Creation's Physique
therefore my eternal peace
is never breached.

Never On My Knees

Busters have no principles,
Soft as Nicole Carson's nipples,
Death before dishonesty,
It's just that simple,
Cross me 1 time h%,
And I'm more poisonous than lead
In your temple,
They scream the American Dream,
To hell wit that,
It doesn't include you & me,
Everybody wants that mean, mean green,
Broads out there trickin',
Fellas on they knees lickin',
Not even the crumbs from da beast,
Psychologically destroying themselves, you & me,
The most worst nightmare you can think of becomes unleashed,
Always smilin' 4 da over-rated man,
Getting set out like Playboy Pam,
Jolly cause you left Hollywood paid,
2 many black celebrities are rubber-made,
You're nothing more than a 21st century slave,
Put an outlaw fo' life on my grave,
White, Black, Jew it don't matter no more,
Bit$#@% str8 selling they souls,
While integrity & Black Pride are left at the door,
Forget being played like a game of dice,
Fu#$ wearing knee pads for life,
Da@% the price!
H%s you'll have to take my life.

GughD Niitte

Rest well my angel
Relax your thoughts
No worries tonight
It'll all work out
Dream on dream on
Where will we meet this time?
Just close your eyez
Let your mind unwind
Your feet are weary
U worked so hard today
While you rest 4 (u) unyielding
Happiness & security I pray
When the sun comes up
We'll tackle this world together
Ok?

TRUMPING A FIXED DECK

Family Photographs

Left to Right: Haneef and Kinda

(L) Charles, Jacque, Lee, and Omar
Background: Christina (sister)

Front: Leslie and Haneef
Back: Naim, Rhonda, and Christina

Asha and Charles

Aunt Donna

Aunt Marcia and little Matt

Front: (L) Elijah and Charles
Middle: (L) Omar, Lee, and Kendall
Back: (L) Hassan, Nadiyah, Jacque, Asha, and Chari

(L) Elijah, Hassan, and Nadiyah

Naim and Haneef

Front: Naim
Back: Christina, Haneef, Rhonda, and Leslie

(L) Uncle Jim, Dad (Dennis Sabree), and Mom (Dolores Sabree)

Mom (Dolores Sabree) and Dad (Dennis Sabree) at Leslie and Julius' wedding

No Mean Muggs

Atmosphere enveloped,
In irresistible hickory smoke,
Insatiable BBQs,
No evening news,
Chari, DeAndre, & Wil
R enjoyin' the invaluable moments,
Doing what they do,
Khalil, Jamie, & Khadeejah
r immersed in the jollity 2,
No singin' the blues,
No pointless glares,
It's all love here,
Incessant laughter,
Where the children,
Nadiyah, Asha, Kerae, and Jalen,
Partake n jubilant palaver,
My encephalon has outreached,
The cloud 9 ladder,
I give the grassroots a hug,
The Amazonian goddess,
Simpers at my oculus tug,
Conversing with my uncle Dan
and aunt Cheryl,
We tip our mugs,
Samplin' heavenly soulfood,
As I take sips from my cup,
Al-Jannah incarnate on earth?
That's what's up.

Dedicated 2: Rasheedah Hanifa

No Time 2 Say Good Bye

We went 2 school 2gether
Off 94 and Van Dyke
My friend had the type of personality: smart, positive, and sociable
That was easy to like
She had the prettiest eyes
& a soft-spoken state of mind
I regret I was forced
To endure a dark moment n tyme
I turned 2 God 2 ask him why
She is sparklin' wonderfully
Undetectable by the sophisticated radar pie
Homogenous with the sky
I know she's eternally smillin'
A zillion miles high
I just wish I had the opportunity
2 say Good Bye.

Dedicated to: Mr. Reeves

Photo Finish

Photographically impressed
The eye contact & strong handshakes
The meaningful conversations
Or important calendar dates
And those masterful pictures he would effortlessly take
Travelled a thousand miles to see me
Graduate
That fact
The most potent words still understate
An authentic pioneer
In this game
We call life
Fully equipped with class and sagacity
A real man
A debonair.

Oblivious 2 Change

The current administration to the health of my city,
Is worse than HIV,
But that's what the people decided 2 support,
Rather than vote for me,
U can't keep enabling & exhibiting the same behavior or actions then expect different results,
That's insane,
When I ran for city council,
My pledge was to promote and facilitate positive change,
Residents cry and complain,
Regarding prevalent conditions ordained,
Concurrently leaving my pledge 2 brutally hang.
Opting 2 not give me or the soulja Hank a single chance,
Double-crossed by the ones who recommended my stance,
Then they naively wonder why the younger generation doesn't respect their elderly glance,
All Hampton & his sycophants have ever done,
Is sing & prance,
The enemy converges on the city,
Inkster residents are disenfranchised,
Levied usurious taxes,
& the community finishes last,
Jerking the election is representative of their past,
Nothing u can say,
because u voted 4 their as#.

TRUMPING A FIXED DECK

Good Guy Gott Got

Part I
These chicks say they ain't
 caught up n da cash
Yeah he dresses suave
Talks smooth
 His ride is clean
 Crib's on "lean"
 & on a daily he be beatin' dat a#%

 Eyes lookin' like a raccoon's mustache
 "It's not about the flash"
 "It ain't about the cash"
 Only words you speakin' is trash
Tail str8 gettin' smashed
A true dude step real 2 u
 & that cat is grass
 Transformed into an a$#
 Facial expression is crass
 So much 4 all the time and money u spent in da past

The kids aren't yours,
 Besides I don't want u no more
 I was just gankin' yo a%#
Thank you though 4 everything
Including the "bling",
 Especially those diamond rings
Did I mention
I have some new niggas on my team
Thanks 4 all that u do
But nigga u a fool
Because I was only playin' you.

Part II
"Why do good girls choose bad boyz?"
"Why these broads use real men 4 toyz?"
"A good man is hard to find"
"Your man was committed 2 u"
"Why u let that busta dude tap it from behind?"
Make that fatal mistake & treat her too kind
New name acquired will be monkey shine
You'll look like those investors for Enron
Who got robbed savagely blind
Like a venomous snake you got bit repeatedly
As if by design
"Homie!" Game over
B4 the end of this rhyme
Slews of chicks
Have unmatched trixs
Deception & talk
Yeah u walk that walk
Line 4 line,
Sick of (triflin') women cryin' & whinin'
Time after time
Mouth & character so maligned
Do yourself a big favor
Give dat grill & soiled appeal
A triple whop
"No baby I love you"
"I must ask you why?"
"Girl shut up with the lies!"
Cause good guy got dropped
Good guy got popped
Good guy gott got
Left forsaken 2 stand
With his di$k n his hand.

unbrakdounabowl

Securely anchored is my will,
As if it weighed a million tons of steel,
If my life gets spilled,
Then that's the price I have to pay,
4 my shorties to grow up strong,
Every night I pray,
Being a true man is far greater,
Than any money figure,
I won't bow down,
To those who try to play me 4 a nigger,
Get your own riches,
Never settle for (any) leechin' bi#$?@%
Everyone's entitled to a piece of the pie,
So why are you trippin' off mine,
When I'm tryin' to survive,
Countless souljas have died,
After jealousy and tempers collide,
And when I become a donor to the hearse,
My young gunz,
Will have inherited,
The earth.

TRUMPING A FIXED DECK

DEDICATED TO: BABA

UNDENIABLE TRUTH

DATING BACK SINCE I WAS A LIL' YOUTH,
U PROVIDED AN **EVER**LASTING ROOF,
WITHSTANDING UNCOUNTABLE PEOPLE & SITUATIONS,
WHO FIT THE TITLE OF UNCOUTH,
ALWAYS FIRM BUT SHOWED MUCH LOVE THROUGH & THROUGH,
PUT THE FAMILY BEFORE SELF & WEALTH 2,
SPENT ENDLESS TIME,
2 DEVELOP THE MIND,
AND POSITIVE ENERGY,
THAT'S U,
THE WISEST KING I EVER KNEW,
WHETHER IT'S HELPING 2 SOLVE MATH PROBLEMS,
THROWIN' A FOOTBALL,
COORDINATING FAMILY GATHERINGS @ THE PARK,
OR TYING A SHOE,
EQUATABLE TO A RARE EMERALD,
AGELESSLY NEW,
BATMAN & SUPERMAN ARE FANTASY,
THE MAN THEY CALL "THE TRUTH,"
WITHOUT QUESTION OR DEBATE,
IS FOREVER TRUE.

Can't Let It Rydd

Why those tricks kill my auntie
Cognitions of murderin' the culprits
In cold-blood still haunts me
2 my Aunt Ruth, Aunt Donna,
Uncle Jim & Andrew
2 name a few
4 the 1s I've lost
The gardens they flew

To my grandfathers I never knew,
I'll see u in the pearly sky
That I promise u

I wish my godbrother didn't take his own life
Never had a chance to tell him
Hold on Baby, It'll be alright,
They merked "My Nigga,"
and left him n the snow
This transpired (shortly) after 84',
Till this day the so called law
Never got those h%$
I'm not tryin' 2 hear peace no more

My boy 'A-Juice' didn't deserve that fate
His life bit#%
U had no right to take

We'll hook up again at heaven's gate
So much pain I can't escape
Revenge and rage I cogitate
The world too busy until my wake

TRUMPING A FIXED DECK

My mind screamin' for dat' .38
A child growin' without a father
Breeds a heavy plate

Unyielding traffic merged
Upon a damaged slate
Walls of bliss degenerate

Permanent shelter is seeked
In confidence I generate
I'm on the edge man
Jugglin' w8
Lord please forgive me
4 the sins I make.

Neva My Fate

I thought about leavin',
But spendin' an eternity n Hell,
Could neva b my fate,
Scores of people luv me,
That would b a detrimental, irreversible mistake,
I must c Lil' Sanaa ameliorate,
In spite of (all) the anguish,
She imparts a clairvoyant cape,
The agony can't b conceptualized,
It's in advance of one's mental landscape,
As I speculate,
Why did it have 2 b my heart she mauled?
Even though the efforts rendered,
Covered wall 2 wall,
Man,
This world don't give a fu#$ about a nigga,
Just waitin' on my downfall.

Humble Got Shot

A horde of cats are brought up
with a silver spoon in their mouth,
But that's not what life is all about,
Head blown up bigga than the Dirty South,
Thinkin' they're God's gift to the entire world,
Character more phony than a 2 dollar curl,
It's enough to make you wanna hurl,
Imperative that you tell the corrosive ills,
Of boastfulness & cockiness to your lil' girl,
To always respect those who might not be doing as well,
So her mind will continue to blossom,
And gel.

Tru Retrospect

In retrospect of history,
Society too frequently alleges I don't have 1,
But through my ancestors the first civilizations & forms of government begun.
In retrospect of history,
All those inventions you use every single day,
Imagine what life would be like if they remained tucked away.
In retrospect of history,
We use to network and operate as one community,
Now due 2 brainwashing "I have mine you get yours" is the new immunity.
In retrospect of history,
Textbooks consistently construct timelines starting at slavery,
The audacity to upkeep that fallacy still amazes me.
In retrospect of history,
Unyielding physical, emotional, and psychological battles endured,
Resulting in the blood of courageous & mighty souls being poured.
In retrospect of history,
You'll embark on descendants of Kings and Queens such as Imhotep, Akhenaton, Hatshepsut and Nefertari,
Which ignited a rich and illustrious tradition far from theory.
In retrospect of history,
Conceptualize a tree stabilized by its roots,
Distort history and that same tree becomes weak and loose.

I Thought We Was Cool

We were tight since primary school,
Why you switch on me dude?
I thought we was cool.
We used to play "Kill Da Man,"
You was like my brotha back then,
Poppin' "Jays" in the backyard,
Flexin' like some young starz,
How could everything change so hard,
I thought we was cool.
Why did jealousy and tribulation have to spool,
U flipped cliques on me too,
U were my main man dude,
I thought we was cool.
If cats tried to put a gauge hole n my back,
Or if I had to scrap,
You would leave da homie flat,
That's an "out cold" stat,
Cause I thought we was cool.

The Cards I was Dealt

Prosperity & tranquility I dream of,
But there's so much to jostle wit',
If I don't provide,
The riches & charm,
Will I lose out,
Like a what if,
The world is filled with so much hate,
Deceit, immorality & trickery,
Flood my gates,
What will my lady do,
If I don't come thru,
Could it be all she wrote,
Played out by a stranger,
Or a cat I knew,
I try not to mess with all that stress,
But every day I wake,
There's always another test,
So however it plays out,
I'll do my very best,
I can't be dissuaded by all the rest,
The simple things in life are often overlooked,
Don't make the mistake & read me like a nursery school book,
I never inspired 2 be a movie star,
Nor drive (around in) 20 fancy cars,
Like DP I just want to be free,
To be who I want to be.

Alltahm

Changin' days are b4 us,
Brite moments lie ahead,
In an array of splendor the leaves have shed,
Thru a multitude of colors,
You'll find diversity has spread,
The winds of the season once had led,
Flowers & ferns have returned 2 their steads,
With an abundance of vigor,
Gourds of beautification,
Thru creation,
Is read.

President 4 the People

I never considered being
Republican or Democrat
Because they're both rats
Same destination
Just different paths,
If u beg 2 differ
Look at the Constitution
The Trans-Atlantic Slave Trade
The penal or judicial system
And for over 4 hundred years
The treatment of blacks
America was going under
If it wasn't 4 the exchange
The pivotal change
With his signature authenticity and charisma
Dedication 2 major issues and morality
Upon the inauguration of Barack
As an angelical "close-out" pitcher
He saved the game
He has restored America's name
If I could only get my young comrades 2 switch
Their mind frames
see it isn't what they claim
it's not what it seems
young seeds want 2 b like *Scarface
but I let them know that sort of thinking is green
if u want 2 b like somebody
inspire 2 be President Barack Obama
he far more than epitomizes
big dreams & aspirations 2 follow
4 our leaders of 2morrow.

*pigeon-hearted Cuban gangster from the movie screen

Rainbow Lynn

Ever go for a stroll,
After a winter snow,
Stopped to watch the joy in a kid's eye,
On the merry-go,
Or captured the beauty,
As a flower grows,
You are truly loved,
I wanted to let you know,
Just in case I never told you so,
Whether it's your pleasant ego,
Or your internal makeup so colorful,
Tranquil like a river flow,
My "gyrl" 4 life,
No doubt,
Fo' sho',
Before I let you go,
My words to you,
A queen I know.

Respect Affiliated

To the homies,
Fred, Los, Larry, & Mickey,
Da game stays tipsy,
It's time to get that cho,
Are u wit me,
Nothing of lasting worth,
Comes quickly,
Cats are shallow & papery,
Like a quickie,
To my souljas for life,
Hold it down,
N da "Rock Town",
And holla if you hear me.

Role Modelz

Dating back to the age of the race car tracks,
U watched out 4 me,
As battle catz,
Notable figures,
N a land,
Comprised of serpents, trendsetters, alley, and Aristocatz.

Shine Again

Now I leave you as I (once) came,
I'm not a man of much fortune or fame,
Life can be a confusing game,
You have to corroborate thru the strain,
But never hold your head n shame,
Remember that every day it can't rain,
Because the sun will shine again.

Shortie Got Style

You being my homegirl is cool
No doubt I like spendin' time wit' you
There's no pressure no matter what we do
bottom line my only request
Would be for you to stay tru
Then I'll always come thru
We can go as far as you r willing to go
Fast or slow
I just want you to be happy & comfortable
Recollect our situation is flexible
It don't have to stop on the friend level
Which ever way floats your boat
My ambition is to leave the competition smoked
If you r lookin' for bigga and betta things
I'm your horoscope
I want to take trips with you to Florida & Californian beaches
Travel to places you may have thought you'll never be reachin'
Dip out one day to Venice, The Nile or France
Only thing I'm askin' is can I have this dance?

Dedicated 2: Big Bro

The Dream and I

Every since the start,
You had that spark,
Helped show me the light,
Amidst the evils & temptations of the dark,
A symbol of strength, security, & inspiration,
Like Noah's Ark,
No question u left a mark,
Thru listening and providing a gateway,
When a brotha had somethin' to say,
Rolled out the royal carpet,
If I visited or needed somewhere to lay,
Solidified that irreplaceable connection no matter how far away,
The realest soulja,
I can never repay,
Incomparable merit 2 this very day,
This is str8 from my heart,
Until death do us part,
Brothas from birth,
Until we leave this earth.

TRUMPING A FIXED DECK

Tiger Claw

Tiger Claw Profile
- African American
- Computer Science expert
- Combat & firearm specialist
- Renowned scientist
- 10th degree+ blackbelt
- Communication analyst
- Saved over 2,000 lives
- Immortal
- Dedicated father
- Never lost a single hostage
- Loves soul food

Playin' Against a Fixed Deck

Yeah my spirits are low,
Spent all those years in school,
And don't have nothin' to show,
26 yet still dirt poor,
No money,
No fame,
All I can claim,
Is my 1st, middle, and last name,
And that's a cryin' shame,
Stuck at the end of the totem pole,
Got to have that pad on the beach,
Where the oceans roll,
I hit rock bottom,
Too young to have so many problems,
Maybe I need to grab the revolver and…
I'm tired of playin' the invisible figure man,
Majority not caring whether I'm livin' or dy-in',
Society & the world will never fully
Understand da man that I am,
But (u know) I really don't even give a dam$.

Souljas Can You Hear Me

As I lay down to sleep,
I think about the cold harsh streets,
The millions dangling,
Cause they can't make ends meet,
Far too many swaying like a raggedy leaf,
Big head blacks get money & prestige,
So they think I'm beneath,
Tryin' to fit in with Uncle Sammy, Bob Dole,
Annie, or Bush…,
While all along being viewed,
As a nigger on a leash,
You wonder why I can't sleep,
Brothas killing brothas,
Schools killing brothas,
Gov't killing brothas,
Brothas encompassing Ms. Americas,
And sistas turning to someone other,
Ain't that a muthaf$#&?%,
Our history appears to be lost, stolen, or strayed,
There's more than enough pain,
To drive an honorable soulja insane,
But that's the name of the game,
That may sound like a sad thang,
However the world is far from clean,
If you're weak,
There's no way you can hang,
I'm a soulja til' I die,
Representin' fo' life the "Crooked I",
I won't turn back,
I won't give in,
I will not surrender,
I will not bend,
To all my souljas,
It's time to mount up,
For all my enemies,
You're s#$% out of luck.

Dedicated to: Kinda

K 2 Da' A

If someone tried 2 hurt her
Dearly they would pay
I know I ain't no killa
But the AK will spray
I pray my wife 1 day
Will b symmetric 2 her
N a number of ways
I love her to death man
I put that on my life
There's no need 2 ask the homie twice
To my cuz
My soulja
My comrade
Thru thick & thin
There's so much positive to say
Cause she's the K 2 Da' A.

The Young Lady Off Brooklane

Pure as a mother's baby,
Yet able to sparkle like a gust of light,
A symbol of deep beauty and originality,
As thou a calm wind on a summer night,
Truly special indeed,
But unlike the golden book,
Which is often judged by its cover,
I smile when I see her,
A real Egyptian Queen.

Words of a Soulja

My life hasn't been the best,
Only a few have survived upon leaving the nest,
There's always jokes about the ghettos and pens,
But I don't see not one thing funny,
Especially when my homie just got smoked fo' less than money,
It's like walking a balance beam,
Without a day's worth of training,
Which eventually can become physically and mentally draining,
But something deep down won't let me quit,
Even though the drama is getting way too thick,
Will I grow old?
Seems a cloudy thought,
Since every new day another brother has dropped,
Regardless thou the true power in knowledge must be sought,
Real honor and recognition can never be bought,
As a young brotha eludes being outlined in white chalk.

Who Am I?

I'm a Zula warrior,
A pure flame burner,
A str8 Nat Turner & Mau Mau descender,
I'm not a bull-shi%$er,
I'm a no quitter,
A home run hitter,
A str8 go-getter,
I eat pessimist, naysayers & haters
4 dinner.

Dedicated to: Yahmi and the hard working/
underappreciated women of the world

Wonda Woman

Above the constant hardships & barriers foes generated,
In the end you always had "them faded,"
Every single day,
U paved a way,
So your seeds would be laced,
Proud of the skin they're in,
Standing tall & strong,
At the same time managing studies, bills, and your own,
It's quite obvious u da bomb,
Nothin' short of a supa mom,
Upon nights of pain & sorrow,
It was difficult to see a better tomorrow,
But u maintained composure & persevered,
With tranquility like a sparrow,
Piercin' through parasites, rattlers, & cowards,
U touched another level,
& you do it with "madd" style and grace,
1 can only revel,
I know u r a "fine" regal human,
Betta known as,
Wonda Woman.

TRUMPING A FIXED DECK

Dedicated to: Roy

Where Ever U R

Where ever U r,
Are u alright?
Remember we took that trip to Ohio to see "The Dream?"
And (the) 5.0. tried 2 aggravate our team,
Even the K-9 unit became part of the theme,
They didn't know or care,
That we roll squeaky clean,
Notwithstanding the patrol being trite,
The event was still "Top Flight,"
When I hook up with the 2 of u,
It's trump tight,
You're not only a cousin,
More so a brother 2 me,
If I never told u,
U r my dude,
A stand up cat,
This isn't a generic rap,
To my big cuz,
I just hope u r alright,
Where ever u r.

Ruptured Heart

I envisioned it was 4 keeps
from the start,
So how could she just crush my heart,
2 love & not sincerely be loved in return,
Stings worse than any internal 3rd degree burn,
From her I saw seeds filled with laughter,
But in reality my spirit got shattered,
She was treated like the last queen on this
earthly platter,
But she walked away coldly,
After all that memorable time,
Like it didn't even matter,
Settled for a chump who previously played her,
Deceived & faked out like a pack of "now & laters",
The fiery love in me 4 her created,
Became terminally deflated,
The love she said was there 4 me was n actuality dilapidated,
Travelled to the ends of the earth,
So what we had wasn't dissipated,
My card North Memphis played it,
She made the bed,
Now her a$# has to lay in it,
2 the one I sacrificed far more
than my part,
Yet she ruptured my heart.

Ever Ask Why

Why do a large number of whites think I'm a nigger
Why do so many blacks try to burn me like a cinder
Why they get animalistic on Emmitt Till
What's up wit' Arabs shootin' and bashin' brothas wit tire irons for a thrill
Ever figure out why da' chinaman stays on ill
Why r insurance companies so cannibalistic as they
Prey on the young & old collimate 2 Jack & Jill
Why as long as it doesn't concern them they say chill
Why my comrade Pac get his cap peeled
Explain how brothas clashing n da street = blood distilled
What made Marvin Gaye's father take his only son with a kill
Why every time u down that alcohol u break a governmental seal
How did God get replaced by Ms. Cocaine & Mr. Pill their kids' lust & dollar bill
Tell me
Why life have to be this way
Where great martyrs such as Malcolm X, Martin, and Medgar
Get conspired upon and murdered thru (*) the CIA
How come I can't find peace when I rest
Why America have to go/run around the world with a poked out chest
Why is my best unable to pass society's tests
When will Blacks stop allowing religion to cause so much divisive stress
How come sistas and brothas can't avoid the unnecessary friction
Since our ancestors the Egyptians represented the utmost in unified precision
How did the world end up in such a crazy disposition
To the point where despicables just up and violate our children
Why situations got my people in such an awkward position
What the hell is going on with all the gay renditions
How can I end all the head on collisions
Why the real criminals start within the governmental system
Do you really like what you see in the mirror

Is the image any clearer
Be cautious of the mirages
Fostered by (none other than)
The daily news and the media
Sellin' gimmicks and false pretenses
Like www.expedia.

(*) COINTELPRO &

Ladi Chi

Worthy of being recognized in high esteem,
Rank nothin' short of an Original Queen,
Promise me u will never let anyone kill your beautiful spirit or dreams,
U have a brotha's back,
Betta than the A-Team,
Any competitors,
U blew them off the scene,
No other woman has been so down 4 me,
Deep down u have me wantin' to do anything,
If u eva r in need,
Call on me by all means,
I put that on everything,
Not only are u so real & intellectual,
But u r a pretty young thang.

Put Your Fists ↑

The elders probably won't approve of what I wrote n these lines,
Please excuse me,
I had to say what's on my mind,
President Clinton, Reagan & the brethren symphonized global counterproductive deviations,
Exasperated thru the anterior receiving oral copulation n the White House,
& it was swept under the rug,
Roethlisberger is the poster boy 4 sexual assault charges,
& Goddell coddles him with a hug,
U can b an infidelic adulterated governor,
But if u fit the mode of the "Terminator,"
The status of the ghoulistic media is unplugged,
What the fuc$,
My brothas Kwame Kilpatrick & Michael Vick,
Got legally lynched,
All the greatness they accomplished,
1 revolutionized a game,
1 resuscitated a major city,
Both galvanized beyond the bounds of a plethora,
Per mendacity & exaggerated counter activity,
(the public bought n 2 it),
"they" attempted 2 wipe them out,
N a cinch,
Poor gettin' poorer,
& the rich get rich,
The welfare of the people is voted insignificant,
Ain't that a bitc#,
Put up your fists,
N contempt of the preponderance of evidence,

TRUMPING A FIXED DECK

The cost of my plea,
2 Judge Victory,
Is covered,
N a cent.

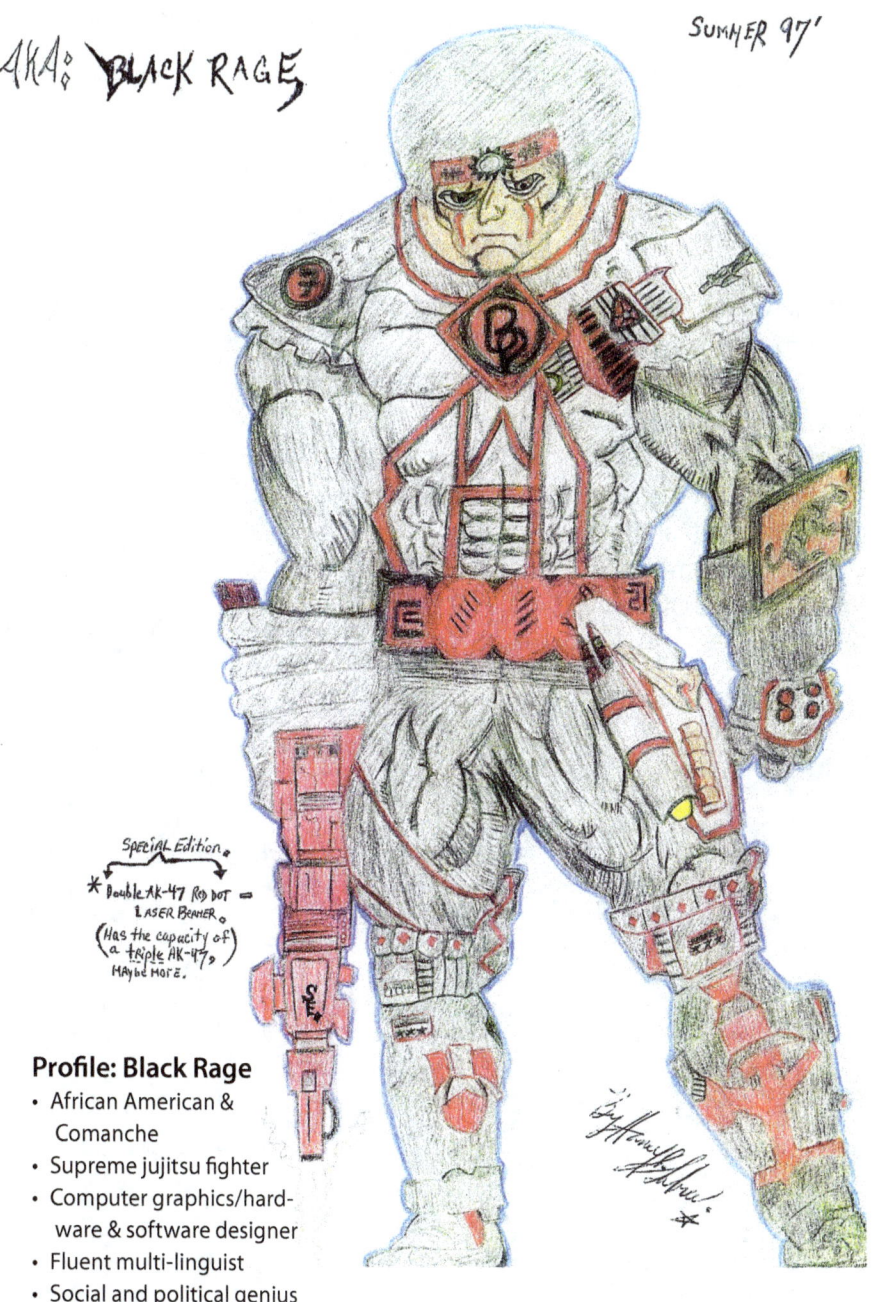

Profile: Black Rage
- African American & Comanche
- Supreme jujitsu fighter
- Computer graphics/hardware & software designer
- Fluent multi-linguist
- Social and political genius
- Extreme naturalist
- Global revolutionary
- Weapons/laser perfectionist

TRUMPING A FIXED DECK

Dedicated to: My Boy From 1585

Acec of Spadez

Bionic Commando and aviation simulations,
Used 2 b his games,
If there is an enshrinement 4 my Generals from the Bloc,
He would b n the Hall of Fame,
Smashin' Frosted Flakes 2 concrete tops,
Watchin' Saturday cartoons 2 kick-off @ noon,
That was our thang,
21 gun salute my brotha,
With a Sawed Off bang.

R199

MUZIC CAN B MIND CONTROL,
MONITOR THE CONTENT & BANGIN' BEATZ
U FEED YOUR BRAIN,

CANNIBUS & CELL PHONES HAVE THE
YOUNG GENERATION PIMPED & SEVERELY
SMOKED,
DÉ JÀ VU FROM THE 60s',
QUALIFYING FOR A JOB IS COMATOSE,

LIVIN' A LIFE OF CAPITAL STANDARDS
& SUBSTANCE,
NO PRICE TAG IS A FEASIBLE MATCH,

SELECTING 2 ELOPE TRUE TO ONES SELF
IN ABANDONMENT,
FORFEITURE EVENTUATED N SELF RE-
SPECT,
THE DISPOSSESSION OF ALL CREDIBILITY
IS HATCHED,

NONETHELESS B THANKFUL 4 EACH NEW
BEGINNING,
BECAUSE SOMEWHERE SOMEONES CHAPTER MET
ITS END,
U HAVE BEEN GRANTED ANOTHER CHANCE TO
FIGHT ONCE AGAIN,
MUSTERING UP ENOUGH MENTAL FORTITUDE 2
RISE UP FOR THE FIGHT,
COMPRISES THE DOMINANT PERCENTAGE OF THE WIN.

TRUMPING A FIXED DECK

Frozen in Time

Short Stories

The Journey Within

Some people believe that once a person has gone astray there is little or no chance for progressive change. It's important to make a distinction between personal opinions and matters of fact. With hope perseverance is possible, without it the battle is over before it begins. A defeated hopeless mind-set can become a volatile game of Russian roulette; superseding any other determinant, if progressive change is to occur it must begin with the man/woman in the imager.

It was a late Monday morning on November 27th. Maleek was awakened by a breeze that slipped pass his opened bedroom window; the aroma of hot blueberry pancakes, scrambled eggs with Provolone, and sizzling turkey sausage further revived his five senses. As he gazed out the window the air outside was calm, cool and pleasant; it was similar to the touch of a cashmere pillow after an extended day of drudgery. Birds of hue were flying gracefully cutting through the atmosphere as a razor blade on paper. Across from the huge towering casas you could see gently rolling hills and an overabundance of greenery. Miles and miles of trees made of oak and evergreen could be spotted gasping with life. Rose Moss, ferns, and Begonias of such beautiful delight captured the scene. Nevertheless, there arrives a point in time when we have eyes but we fail to see…

Maleek, alias is MT, had just finished eating a hearty breakfast and was preparing for school at Reginald Lewis High. He threw on his dark jeans, casual designer shirt, and suede black Rockport shoes. Every day he would wear one of his sacred necklaces which carried great meaning. The rotation of jewelry consisted of an ankh, Egyptian symbol for everlasting life, a silver necklace given to Maleek on his sixteenth birthday, and one with predominantly black beads except some beads had the colors red, yellow, and green. The colors in the last piece of jewelry mentioned were symbolic: black—pride and respect for self, red—sacrifice, hard work, and blood that was spilled during trying times, yellow—natural riches (not fancy cars or dead presidents but wonders from the ancient lands of Africa, priceless minerals/resources), and green—the vibrant, luscious land. Today Maleek chose the necklace with the beads; no protocol was his motivation it was all about spontaneity.

Maleek was approaching Reginald Lewis High and began to laugh to himself. He often admired the aesthetics of this four floor masterpiece, especially the state of the art media center. Once Maleek made it to school he spoke with his good friend Darrick in the hallway before class. Darrick, nickname is D, was slender built, brown-skinned and well respected. They grew up in the same neighborhood, practically lived at each other's house, and stuck together like glue through thick and thin. He and Maleek were brothers for life.

The school week went by swiftly and the weekend had finally arrived. Before he could hang with his friends or run some errands Maleek needed to complete his Saturday chores. With the help of his brother Rakkim they were able to finish building a sophisticated patio for their mother and father. This was the second Saturday for the project, but now Rakkim and Maleek could enjoy the fruits of their labor. Rakkim was a born craftsman; consequently the job went along quite smoothly. Most of the plans for the construction were done on Rakkim's Dell Inspiron laptop utilizing CAD (Computer Aided Design) software.

Maleek's parents and family loved him; he was truly one of a kind. He had a beautiful intelligent girlfriend and his reputation at school was a monster truck. There was one particular though, Maleek sometimes lived life as a NASCAR driver. Everyone has problems of their own; but do you know what hurt Maleek the most? He was stubborn at times and neglected to look over situations carefully before taking action. What he failed to realize was a hard head will get a young brother dead.

The next scene takes place on school grounds after dismissal for Thanksgiving Break.

Time had begun to catch up with Maleek, and when it did he felt it.

"Maleek! Wait up; I need to speak with you for a minute. Man, I'm beginning to worry about you bro," says Darrick.

"Ah, Darrick you don't have to worry about me, I'm going to be alright," Maleek replied.

Kalawno is known by many as K-Lo.

"Then why have you been hanging around that sinister named Kalawno, he's more crooked than a coat hanger. Is he one of your boys' now? And what about last week MT? We were suppose to drop by Keisha's birthday party, what happened? Not to mention, the school-wide talent show is right around the corner and you haven't made it to one practice session; the crew wants to know what's going on."

"D you're confused man I'm out of here," said Maleek shaking his head as he walks away.

"Maleek the only person confused is you, the sooner you realize that the better!" Darrick yelled behind him.

Over the Thanksgiving Break and Christmas holiday Maleek's association with Darrick and the rest of his crew became progressively worse. His girlfriend, Tamara, was very concerned because he continued to act out of character.

It was January 1, 1998 the beginning of a new year. The huge pools of water at the perimeter of the town were ice blue and the tempestuous weather was becoming quite frigid. The environment appeared pastoral; you could hear the cry of a cathedral mouse. Maleek was suppose to be with his friends at a college prep workshop. All the same, the glitz, glamour, and swagger K-Lo and his clique provided had MT too far gone. Tamara, D, and the crew were old news now.

Night had begun to set in, and the environed area appeared to be desolate. The bright golden rays from the street lights were the only element that kept the district from total darkness.

The neck of the woods where Maleek was about to pass through wasn't known for deconstructive activity and mischievous nighttime opportunists. But recently the situation had totally changed unbeknownst to him.

MT continued to walk with K-Lo and his clique. They conversed about the eye candy at the mall from earlier, the clean gear they picked up, big dreams, and fast money. Maleek was so engaged in the dialogue that he forgot a cardinal rule: observe the surroundings at all times. Click! Click!

"You know what time it is. Drop your money, jewelry, and wallets on the ground! Make it quick, unless you want to die tonight." At gunpoint Maleek and the others practically forfeited everything except the clothes on their back.

"You cats are ghosts, this isn't over! Dead you hear me! Dead!" said Kalawno.

That comment by Kalawno was a costly mistake. The assailants rushed their victims and begin pistol whipping them with the blunt end of their pearl handled pieces, in a state of pure mania. Several members resisted fiercely, but their efforts were futile. To say the attackers didn't discriminate would be an understatement.

As the gunmen are about to leave, one of them steps up to Kalawno, cocks his weapon and presses the cold steel against Kalawno's cranium.

"Loose lips sink ships, boss man."

As the gunman begins to walk away, one of Kalawno's boys drew his Beretta. Nevertheless when he attempted to fire it, it jammed.

"Damn!"

The air rang out with boundless fury. "Pop! Pop!" "Bbddhhah! Bbddhhah!" just like that; when the smoke cleared the air transformed from placid to dreary as Jeckel and Hyde. A few people were wounded. Kalawno and one of his boys' got hit first. But they were lucky. Their injuries weren't life threatening. Everyone who was with Maleek scurried away from the scene. The gunmen left as quickly as they arose.

On the wintriness heartless pavement laid MT. He was motionless, bleeding profusely, and fading in and out of consciousness. The sound of sirens consumed the night hour.

The ambulance is at the scene. An EMT and paramedic tend to Maleek first.

"Whoever called this one in, may have given the young man a slim chance of survival, a paramedic said. Otherwise this incident had DOA written all over it. A few more minutes and I don't know if he would have made it to the ER."

As the EMTs hoist Maleek into the ambulance, one exclaims, " Ok! We're all set, let's move!"

Upon giving Maleek medical attention (i.e. Ivs) in the back of the ambulance, a paramedic thinks to himself: a simple act of courage, a phone call, could be the deciding factor in whether he lives or dies.

It wasn't that he was robbed, but the real downfall was the uncertainty of whether Maleek would live. His life had flashed before him. According to the doctors he had less than a thirty percent chance of recovery. The MD's diagnosis stemmed from a series of tests and the fact that he lost so much blood.

It was a miracle, eight weeks later Maleek was on his way to complete recovery. By his own will, he wanted to re-evaluate his life, analyze it, and develop into the (young) man he was destined to be—mannerable, credible, humble, and great. He decided it was time to go on a reflective journey. Not your typical sort of travel, but a spiritual renewal—a journey within.

The road to self-recovery is tough, plain and simple. It has to start and end with you. Keep in mind, you can't expect to get different results if you do what you have always done. Furthermore if you pray, remain optimistic, determined, and resilient a positive change is inevitable.

In the next paragraph Maleek continues his physical and mental recovery at home.

Three additional weeks passed, the injuries received previously were healing nicely. New places were viewed, landmarks of allurement were pictured. *Unlike* before the power of nature entrapped his mentals. Brother Maleek was constantly in a period of deep thought. He understood that the problem was within himself. After extreme cerebration, MT came to the conclusion that the only means to improve his life was through: faith/hope, a staunch comprehension in the power of God, and a deep belief in the value of life. He knew he came within a thread of death.

It was difficult for quite some time, because that's the nature of change. Remaining steadfast and disciplined with his spiritual-self posed the greatest challenge because it was never routine for Maleek.

Tamara began visiting Maleek on a regular basis offering encouragement and a rock to lean on. Her smile alone could light up a coliseum. Darrick revitalized their communication by involving the two of them in more upbeat activities—bowling, shooting pool, and extracurricular events at school for example. The rest of the crew followed suit soon after. Tamara and D displayed their biggest support by setting a positive example through their behavior.

While at home Maleek had serious dialogue with his parents and true friends. His true friends were those who were with him through thick and thin. Not the ones who came around during the sunshine escaping the rain. Maleek learned a painful lesson; never take something invaluable for granted, because one day you might lose it.

The True Man of Steel

The following events are in no way an adaptation of the current government. This story takes place prior to President Barack Obama's Administration.

In an era where the days seemed desolate and unyielding, the looming nights appeared consuming and uncanny. No one knew what the following days would bring. Evil seemed to have the forces of good on the threshold of oblivion. Politics was before principle, pleasure preceded prayer, money replaced morals, and self-pride transformed into self-hate.

Housing projects were dispersed all over the North American hemisphere. These housing quarters supposedly came into existence to support the less fortunate, but the bottom line is they were just what the name states, projects. Public housing was never intended to place those who need it in a favorable position to achieve autonomy and industriousness. Therefore, since the motives of state/local agencies are skewed, their actions perpetuate stagnation and negative conditions.

Hope was becoming a distant thought and all acts of piety appeared to be for naught. These trying times were felt everywhere irregardless to race, status, or creed. From the ashes rose an illuminating star; not a star from the celestial skies above, but one in human form. Truly a testament of perseverance for his rocky, traumatic past would have buckled the strongest man. Folklore has it that he was a descendent of the legendary Samson. On the contrary, no known historian has decrypted what is true and what is a tall tale. If this mysterious warrior is anything like his predecessor, then once again the forces of evil have met their match.

Relentlessly driven by a divine obligation to his ancestors who lost their lives and whose blood was shed into the waters in which rivers of eternity flow (an infinite number of valiant champions were killed at sea during slave revolts; some even jumped overboard because they chose to face the sharks rather than remain in bondage. When the physical no longer had the breath of life, then through the ocean(s) the spirits returned to heaven). A new dawning has unfolded.

Through the miraculous formation of his existence in connectivity to his extraordinary mental prowess, his strength is unparalleled, his agility highly fluid, the kinetic energy he possesses has no bounds, and his will is a fierce blazing sun. The star's origin, age, and background are unknown. He stands over six feet tall with bronze chiseled features and hair black as the night. Battle after battle, time after time he became known as World Star, Defender of the Earth.

Every year as part of their family tradition the Kamau's would have an elder speak to the children about great stories that had been preserved for over a century; the stories spoke of truth, purpose, and unspeakable fascination. From the comforts of their pristine abode the tender eyes gathered around. On this particular afternoon, curiosity and attentiveness selfishly ravaged the moment:

"Mama Siti was there ever really a person named World Star? Ma'am, well the reason I asked is because TJ from down the street said that World Star was just a name that people made up and that I was going to get in big trouble if I kept telling fables," said Omari excitedly.

"Baby, I'll tell you this much, the man they call World Star was no myth. He was and still is as real as it gets. Sit back little ones and let Mama Siti enlighten you." *When she began telling the story all the children drew in closer.*

There was this one syndicate years ago that nearly pulled off a horrific scheme of mass destruction and control across the nation. Before the assault there was a final assembly, by which a special agent and commander were present.

"For those who are not aware, I'm Special Agent Ravager. This is a masterful plan. With the government tied up in foolish war gibberish, foreign relations faltering, and a weakened economy the timing couldn't have been better. Those simpletons will never meet all our demands, so the hostages will perish."

"Listen up!" *Special Agent Ravager stepped back so the commander could address the army.* "We are to attack the designated targets you see indicated by the red dots on the digital projection; once all points are neutralized, Operation Constrictor is in effect. Are there any questions? Very well, this is Commander Duce Damaja this meeting is adjourned."

The forces of a syndicate called Annihilazion were explosive and domineering.

The upcoming mission is headed by Raincro. As Raincro and his army attempted to exit the FDIC headquarters with hoards of confidential data a band of chivalrous good-doers, The Atomic 5, tried to impede them.

"You harlequins, why waste your insignificant lives. Leave now before I make you regret it!" yelled the villain Raincro, a long time affiliate of the syndicate who had a reputation for being a brutal ruthless antagonizer.

From afar an unfamiliar voice rang out sternly.

"If trouble is what you were looking for then you found it," said World Star.

When the smoke cleared all that remained was artillery shells, damaged buildings, the band of Samaritans (The Atomic 5), and the hero. In the duel between the two giants, (Raincro and the hero), Raincro put up a fight for the ages, nonetheless he soon met his demise. Unfortunately all five members of The Atomic 5 were left in critical condition.

With human-superior vision minutes after his clash with Raincro, World Star made a startling discovery.

The hero was thinking aloud before he bolted effortlessly to the catastrophe.

"There's no sleep for the wicked."

From a far off distance the Zodiac Bridge, a state landmark, began to collapse for no apparent reason. However, the problem was two-fold. A huge oilrig was passing directly below. Like a speed of light the only image visible to the naked eye was a green and blue blur. A sizeable chunk of the bridge fell within an arm's length of the oilrig before the star intercepted it. In using the inert forces of the earth in compliance with his mystical powers the crusader aka World Star mended the monumental bridge back together with flawless precision.

One by one he dismantled all foes that posed a threat to peace on earth. Any diabolical fiend(s) who conspired upon genocide, mental/physical slavery, senseless terror, etc. felt his fury. The evil-ridden bosses endeared the worse punishment. They toppled like dominoes from punches of thunder, flaming kicks, and a barrage of trademark maneuvers: Volcanic Eruption, Soul on Ice, and The Continental Divide. Those were just a few lethal techniques from the defender's massive arsenal.

The aftermath from the warfare formulated an unearthly panoramic, unforgettable indeed. As the days came to pass, the forces of divinity had a new face. Countless encounters were won. However, the war was far from over. In the fiery eyes of the star, World Star, victory was inevitable and defeat was never an option.

Subject Matter: Educational System

Proposal

STATEMENT OF THE PROBLEM AND BACKGROUND

There are a high percentage of African American students who are not prepared to succeed and excel during and after high school.

African American students are not taught satisfactorily about their true history, culture and who they are; thus resulting in low self-esteem, self-respect, and loss of motivation for example. This point, knowledge of self, is the most critical.

Furthermore, far too many students are not gaining the tools and skills necessary to be independent in a global economy and thrive in the real world. For instance, in-depth training in money management, parenting, conflict resolution, communication, etiquette, hygiene and African American studies are essential, yet not fulfilled. The seven points previously mentioned focus on the root of the problem.

The African American student is the highlight of this proposal for a number of reasons:

- There is an alarming percentage of black males imprisoned; this misfortune can be linked to a failed educational system.

- The black student is at the top of the list as far as misrepresentation and academic shortcomings.

- Students are not acquiring the type of schooling vital for mental and social evolvement, which connects to their needs as an African American.

STATEMENT OF THE OBJECTIVES
The objectives below pertain directly to adjustments within the school curriculum and are deemed mandatory:

Two years minimum of African American History
— Black scientists, mathematicians, trailblazers, etc.

Two-part budgeting class within core academia
— For example, Budgeting I, II

Courses in Parenting
— What parenting involves
— Caring for a baby

Conflict Resolution/Communication Classes
— Actions versus consequences
— Guns: melee versus mediation

Etiquette and Hygiene Studies
— Respect for self and others
— Proper ways to care for and conduct yourself

The successful implementation of the above actions will undoubtedly, improve the performance and development of African American students greatly.

How will this be done? Classes in Conflict Resolution for instance, address the issue of gun violence. Students will learn how to disagree without being arguably or violently disagreeable.

Two, courses in Communication target methods for young African American males and females to understand how to converse better in: language, a positive tone and intrapersonal communication with one another.

Through Budgeting courses the students will conceptualize and learn the value of money management. This will give them clear insight on prioritizing needs versus wants.

METHODS FOR DOING THE WORK

— Incorporate the objectives into the school curriculum.

— Provide students and parents with an orientation of the changes at the beginning of the school year.

— Include supplementary workshops to support new changes, (involving parents and students).

— Periodic assessment of teachers and relative constituents within the educational circle, to gauge their performance and efforts in administering curriculum. All parties which have a vested interest in the educational advancement of students need to be held more accountable, *because students rise to the level of expectation.*

Here are a few benefits:

— Increased productivity

— Increased number of well-rounded students

— Motivation and self-worth improved drastically among student body

— Significant growth between relationship of school and home life of students

BUDGET (COSTS) AND SCHEDULE

— Cost is undetermined

— Plan ready for execution after preparatory steps completed

— Continuity/consistency necessary for plan to be effective and ongoing

EXPECTED RESULTS AND EVALUATION PLAN

The modifications suggested, emphasis solutions to serious issues concerning the African American student. If the changes are put into effect, the foundation for learning will strengthen unquestionably.

When the curriculum addresses the overall needs of the students and the working environment is conducive for learning, you have exponential progress.

Just as the European students see reflections of themselves throughout history books and other text, the African American students must know the truth about their ancestry.

The overall student population is the beneficiary of the amended academic program, no matter what their nationality is. The reason being, the new academia provides a broadened educational experience and ties it into real-life situations more interactively.

This proposal will firmly counter numerous hardships and strains that have befallen our African American youth at disproportionate numbers:

— High rates of incarceration

— Teen pregnancy

— Gun violence

— Acts of aggression against one another

— Loss of life

— Low academic achievement

HANEEF SABREE

Parting Thoughts

Kiangazi

Kuanzishwa

*I*f I should lose my life by the hands of one of my own, forgive them for they did that which they knew not. Consequently, in life whether right or wrong you reap what you sow. Therefore, you must do what is right to the best of your abilities and let others think what they will.

As you travel through this world aim for consistency with the simple entities. For instance, treat people with respect and make sure you receive the same. Be considerate not condescending. Exhibiting good manners should be habitual not happenstance. One of the great Prophet's once said, if there was one aspect you should teach your children, its good manners. If you gossip or involve yourself with back-biting strive to break that cycle quick. The participation of back-biting is like eating the flesh of your dead brother.

In a capitalistic society it's imperative to have and make money. But, before the money, be sure to have solid principles as your foundation. Those principles should be grounded in good morals, spirituality, and sound reasoning. The most miserable people tend to be those with the most money. The former clearly illustrates that money cannot buy genuine happiness, trust, commitment, or peace of mind.

Elimu

The synopsis would be unfulfilled if the topic of education was not touched on. What is the true essence of education? I'll let you ponder on that momentarily. The essence of education is not the acquisition of As' in all subjects and receipt of "The Most Likely to Succeed Award." There are critical components necessary for the proper educational development of students. The three I believe are prerequisites of a well-rounded education include: life skills, African American History, and self-sufficiency.

Leading off on the agenda is Mr. and Mrs. Life Skills. I've frequently said a degree and fancy credentials will get you a big time job, but life skills will preserve your vitality. Youth across the nation are grossly deficient in satisfactory life skills. Young scholars of today make excellent grades, however some of their attitudes and manners are undesirable. What good is it to have a great player on your team if he or she is not coachable? What happens when you don't carry the life skills necessary to disagree without being violently disagreeable? There are quite a few intellectuals in the penitentiary and in the grave because they were void of adequate life skills. With proper life skills it creates the balance and understanding of perception and presentation.

Young men, brothers, we have gotten out of control with sagging the pants. It's alright to utilize the belt before you step out into the world. If you check into the origins of sagging pants, you'll find it's a faulty manifestation and represents unmanly attributes. For the ladies, sisters, wearing clothes that displays all your blessings is not attractive. That should be confined to the privacy of your home or alike, for your significant other's eyes only. If you wear clothes which are suggestive, men will approach you with misguided intentions. Personal presentation can create a lasting impression. Regardless to if you're going to an interview or simply running errands, your presentation can make all the difference. You never know who you will meet. I've been told many times, "you never get a second chance to make a first impression."

A multifarious number of students particularly those in urban communities are oblivious to their African American History. If you don't know your history, the foundation is bound for weakness. Not only will you not love yourself, but from a causal relational viewpoint, you in turn will not love your brother or sister. Not knowing about your rich cultured history is undifferentiated from a tree without its roots. This historical teaching will enable young minds to expand knowledge beyond the text book and help them think critically of information that is presented to them.

The ability to think for yourself is underrated, (at school and abroad). We have to get away from "spoon-fed teaching." A shift must take place from dependencies and so-called learning disabilities to self-sufficiency, analyzing, having the confidence to share opinions, independent thinking and trusting ones' self-efficacy (how you feel about your ability to complete a task). When it is all said and done, the true essence of education is to build character and the acquisition of knowledge by Dr. Martin Luther King Jr.

Noda

As men and women we need to start taking the wedding vows seriously. Stop getting married for all the wrong reasons. Recollect that the words you utter before you "jump the broom," are suppose to be taken to heart as well as mind and executed to the fullest extent. If you prefer to "get around", upkeep "friends with benefits" or your predilection is "variety," remain single. Contrarily, when a king finds his queen or vice versa it's similar to having a piece of heaven on earth.

Family life can be a beautiful entity. Marriage at some point should be an essential part of family life. Despite what opponents may project, marriage overall receives a lousy rap. The player, single, and eccentric life style unfortunately tends to supersede the greatness that marriage can be. If you are a player or are trying to become one, rest assured eventually you will get played. Society has defiled the genuine nature of marriage between a man and a woman. The ideas of a union between two individuals are woven into the concepts of procreation. In surveying the creation the laws of magnetism reflect and support the previous statements. Magnets with like charges repel one another. Be that as it may, magnets with dissimilar charges attract. There is a direct correlation to the unison of a man (king) and a woman (queen) with the signs of creation. Human behavior that conflicts, contradicts, and clashes with the natural order can be classified as an abomination.

Imani

To preserve your mental health it's instrumental to have a spiritual religious base. When the world fails you, it is only He that shall never fail you. As long as you maintain a healthy connection with God, in your everyday affairs, no challenge will become too great.

"Remember Him during the good times and He will remember you during the bad times."

~Unknown

Whether you are a Muslim, Christian, Jehovah Witness, etc. only the Creator knows if you're righteous or unrighteous. Being of separate religions doesn't make two people unequally yoked. That sort of backwards thinking is of the slave mind. What is right and morally correct is not based on what church or masjid you attend. The Supreme Judge is God, who created everything regardless of religious affiliation. Society is so expeditious to pass judgment on others when upon looking in the glass prism a hideous reflection appears.

There is only One who knows what is in your heart and if you're going to Hell or Heaven on Judgment Day. Preachers and Imams need to refrain from indoctrinating followers with poison. As religious leaders you need to begin teaching the truth and the word exactly how it is from the holy books, without the apple polishing. Malcolm X said it with succinct clarity, "keep it simple, tell it like it is, and make it plain."

This is an intimation specifically for religious leaders, the like, and for those who the shoe fits; you should cease to impersonate God in conjunction with overstepping your lanes. Because you are not Him and never will be, not even if Hell froze over.

Afya

Brothers and Sisters, people of the world take care of your dietary, physical, and mental health. No matter what your circumstance, make time for yourself alone every day, (at least twenty to thirty minutes). During this time of reflection, contemplate on means to improve your physical health. There are certain types of food that formulate a physical and mental imbalance. Fast food is a major contributor to this imbalance. As a result, it behooves you to stop refueling your body with so much fast food. Fast food places serve food full of chemicals, additives and other ingredients that knock years off of your life. The fast food industry is a formidable adversary to a healthy system. As much as possible, discipline yourself in sticking to nutritious homemade food.

What kind of homemade food? That is the million dollar question. A diet rooted chiefly with fruits, vegetables, certain fish and grains is consummate. Limit the red meat, salt intake, and sugar consumption. Organic foods can be expensive, purchase them when you can (farmer's market is an option). Hydration is essential for health. Drink water consistently daily, leave the pop on the shelf. Your body is roughly seventy percent water just like the earth. We can survive without pop/soda, adversely without water it's check mate.

Be cautious of alcohol and other drugs. Drinking alcohol destroys brain cells, which do not regenerate. Secondly, spirits reverse the conventional cognitive process. Normally rationale is processed before emotions, not when you drink. Other drugs such as marijuana, (aka weed) are overwhelmingly popular. I understand some individuals smoke marijuana because they think it's appealing, whereas others have contrasting reasons why they consume the gateway drug. Whatever the reasons might be, it's not befitting nor is it recommended. Weed is called the "gateway drug;" meaning this destructive drug often leads to more lethal drugs such as cocaine, heroin, methamphetamine, etc. Nothing destroys a people and families like drugs.

Through my research and teaching of Health, it's paramount that you exercise on a regular basis. To endorse the prevention of ailments, diseases, sickness, reduce stress, you name it, the number one recommendation is continual exercise. Those "wonder drugs" and lose weight quick infomercials promote a wonderful lie.

"Reading is to the mind what exercise is to the body."
~Richard Steele

Kutaalamika

When I evaluate the ways of the world and the behavior of the public, I ask myself what is going on. The children and women are exploited, abused and sacrificed with reckless abandonment. It's past time to start loving the children and protecting the women. Malicious behavior towards innocent children and women is debased and a sign of a sick individual. One of a man's central responsibilities is as a protector of the family. Stand up for the children, women, and yourselves. It was once stated by the Honorable Elijah Muhammad, "that for every loose woman there is a man who mistreated her at some point in time." There is substantial merit in that statement.

The most important detail you can spend on a child is time not money. One of my mentor's Dr. V. Johnson, once told me: "children grow into the love they have known."

"All that is needed for the triumph of evil is for good men and women to remain silent and do nothing."

~Edmund Burke

Messages to the reader, before drawing conclusions on information that you may hear or read, collect material from several sources first. The television is a powerful tool; however information the news disseminates is mainly saturated with half-truths, negativity, fear-factor, etc. Discipline yourself to look beneath the surface and weed out the facts from the fiction. My mother used to say, "believe none of what you hear and only half of what you see." Furthermore, if you don't have anything positive to say, it's best not to say anything at all. Optimism over pessimism should be the golden rule. During pre-cultivation my father would stress to me, "think before you speak and act." Those few words transmit incredible wisdom and may save your life one day.

Just because you wear a mean mug, you're spry in firing a flintlock, or are moving steady weight that doesn't make you a gangster. The former characteristics are crippling and extirpating our localities. If your ambitions are to be a gangster or legit trooper, organize our communities, setup businesses in the neighborhoods so that the mighty dollar can circulate in house, a thousand times over. The young generation, women and men should be able to live in their commonalities free of fear, anxiety, and a sense of hopelessness. If you are a part of creating that sort of atmosphere, now that's gangster. True power is in knowledge and wisdom, so stop being paper tigers and step your game up. In the words of Imam Waith Deen Muhammad, "you better wake up and fly right."

References

Books
1. The Holy Quran—A. Yusuf Ali
2. The Bible (Old & New Testament) –World Bible Publishers, Inc.
3. The 40 Hadith –Shaykh An-Nawawi
4. The Bluest Eye –Toni Morrison
5. The Mis-education of the Negro –Carter G. Woodson
6. The Autobiography of Malcolm X –As told to Alex Haley
7. Souls of Black Folks –W.E.B. Du Bois
8. Invisible Man –Ralph Ellison
9. The Road to Memphis –Mildred Taylor
10. Know Thy Self –Dr. Na'im Akbar
11. Conspiracy to Destroy Black Boys –Dr. Jawanza Kunjufu
12. The Rose that Grew from Concrete –Tupac Shakur
13. Autobiography of Assata Shakur –Assata Shakur & Angela Davis
14. Nigger –Randall Kennedy
15. Institutional Racism in America –Louis Knowles & Kenneth Prewitt
16. Surrendered The Rise, Fall, and Revelation of Kwame Kilpatrick –Kwame Kilpatrick
17. Breaking the Chains of Psychological Slavery –Dr. Na'im Akbar
18. From Superman to Man—J.A. Rogers
19. When the Legends Die –Hal Borland
20. No Easy Walk to Freedom –Nelson Mandela
21. Professional Learning Communities at Work—Eaker & DuFour
22. The Alchemist –Paulo Coelho
23. Things Fall Apart –Chinua Achebe
24. 200 + Educational Strategies To Teach Children of Color –Dr. Jawanza Kunjufu
25. Black Indians –William Katz
26. Bury My Heart At Wounded Knee –Dee Brown
27. Stolen Legacy –G. James & A. Hilliard
28. Makes Me Wanna Holla –Nathan McCall
29. Educated to Doom –Bro. Ebby Abdullah
30. Let The Bible Speak –Ali Muhsin
31. To Die For the People –Huey P. Newton

Movies

1. Pride
2. The Great Debaters
3. Malcolm X
4. Something the Lord Made
5. Akeelah and the Bee
6. Hurricane Season
7. Lost, Stolen, or Strayed
8. Eyes on the Prize—Complete Set
9. Roots I—VI
10. The Tuskegee Airmen
11. The Ben Carson Story
12. Tupac Uncensored and Uncut: The Lost Prison Tapes
13. The Last Dragon
14. Cornbread, Earl, and Me
15. Imitation of Life
16. Mooz-lum
17. Black Power Mix Tape 1967—1975
18. Lean on Me
19. Cry Freedom
20. The African History Network: A Great and Mighty Walk
21. The Journey Begins: Tell Me Who I Am (Animated)
22. The Fab Five: ESPN Films
23. The Lion, The Witch and The Wardrobe (Animated, 1979)
24. Bruce Lee Collector's Set
25. Black Belt Jones
26. Three The Hard Way
27. The Wiz
28. Trading Places
29. Coming to America
30. Bilal's Stand

Proverbs

1. *Handling peer pressure/butterflies is like defending a superstar player, you can't stop him/her but you can contain them.
2. "There's no deeper darkness than ignorance." ~ Egyptian Proverb
3. *You have to remove the clouds in order to see the sunshine.
4. "Both tears and sweat are salty, but they render a different result. Tears will get you sympathy; sweat will get you change." ~ Jesse Jackson
5. "Until the lions have their historians, tales of the hunt shall always glorify the hunter." ~ African Proverb
6. "It was not the violence of our enemies but the silence of our friends that we remembered." ~ Dr. Martin Luther King Jr.
7. "Only a fool tests the depths of the water with both feet." ~ African Proverb
8. "Better to light a candle than to curse the darkness." ~ Chinese Proverb
9. "The soul would have no rainbow if the eye had no tears." ~ John Vance Cheney
10. "A setback is a set up for a comeback." ~ T.D. Jakes
11. "In life you either roll on, or get rolled over." ~ Reginal
12. "The truly great man is master of no one and is mastered by no one." ~ Khalil Gibran
13. *A strong foundation will lead to a prosperous black nation.
14. "Sorrow looks behind, worry looks around, and faith looks ahead." ~ unknown
15. "I hope you get what you want, but I hope what you want doesn't get you." ~ J. Harrison Sr.
16. "When you create a new innovative idea, don't worry about the means of presenting it to the world; they will already be trying to steal it." ~ unknown
17. "Don't nothing come to a sleeper, but a dream." ~ anonymous
18. "Smooth seas do not make skillful sailors." ~ African Proverb
19. "Liberate the minds of men and ultimately you will liberate the bodies of men" ~ Marcus Garvey
20. "Talk is cheap it takes money to buy bread." ~ J. Harrison Sr.
21. "Learn politeness from the impolite." ~ Egyptian Proverb
22. "Follow through. Every time you don't do something you said you would do–no matter how small–you lose credibility." ~ E. Lee
23. "You have to be the change you wish to see in the world." ~ Mohandas Gandhi
24. "A lie has many variations the truth none." ~ African Proverb

25. "What is right is not always popular and what is popular is not always right." ~Albert Eistein
26. "One thing I learned about life is it goes on." ~ Robert Frost
27. "The consequences of today are determined by actions of the past. To change your future, alter your decisions today." ~ anonymous
28. "The secret to happiness is to see all the marvels of the world, and never forget the drops of oil on the spoon." ~ Paulo Coelho
29. "If it's not one thing it's another." ~ Great Grandma Harrison
30. "How far you go in life depends on your being tender with the young, compassionate with the aged, sympathetic with the striving and tolerant of the weak and strong. Because someday in your life you will have been all of these." ~ George Washington Carver
31. *For the grass and flowers to grow, the rain sometimes must flow.
32. "Not failure, but low aim is sin." ~ Dr. Benjamin Mays
33. "When you cannot make up your mind which of two evenly balanced courses of action you should take—choose the bolder." ~ William Slim
34. "Never change yourself for anyone; if they don't love you from the start then they will never truly love you." ~ unknown
35. "The darkest hour is just before the dawn." ~ unknown
36. "Care more for the truth than what people think." ~ Aristotle
37. "To die for the racists is lighter than a feather, but to die for the people is heavier than any mountain and deeper than any sea." ~ Huey P. Newton
38. "There's a point where patience ends and cowardice begins." ~ unknown
39. "Do not laugh at the fallen; you may find slippery roads ahead." ~ African Proverb
40. "I would rather die on my feet than live on my knees." ~ Huey P. Newton

*Created by the author

Notable Poems
1. Slow Dance
2. It Couldn't Be Done
3. Who Will Cry for the Little Boy?
4. The Disaster of Negative Thinking
5. Equipment
6. Don't Quit
7. The Road Not Taken
8. Lift Every Voice & Sing
9. Words of Wisdom
10. Attitude
11. If
12. The Power of a Smile

Music
1. Me Against the World—Tupac A. Shakur
2. Gutter Rainbows—Talib Kweli
3. Wake Up—The Roots & John Legend
4. New World Order—Curtis Mayfield
5. Whats Going On—Marvin Gaye
6. Off the Wall—Michael Jackson
7. The Score—The Fugees
8. Innervisions—Stevie Wonder
9. Motown Milestones—The Marvelettes
10. Like Water For Chocolate—Common
11. The Element of Freedom—Alicia Keys
12. Let's Get Free—Dead Prez
13. Black Star—Mos Def & Talib Kweli
14. I Care 4 U—Aaliyah
15. What's the 411?—Mary J. Blige
16. The Best of Diana Ross & The Supremes
17. The Nigger Tape—Nas & DJ Green Lantern
18. Turn Off the Radio Vol. 4—Dead Prez & DJ Drama
19. Aijuswanaseing—Musiq Soulchild
20. Pi Douvan—Orchestre Septentrional Band

21. Buena Vista Social Club—Buena Vista Social Club
22. Nina Simone's Finest Hour—Nina Simone
23. The Scientist—Coldplay
24. Rattle and Hum—U2
25. Gold (Rm)—James Brown
26. The Very Best of Aretha Franklin
27. 2Pacalypse Now—2pac

There's only so much that can be integrated into a single composition. Some accounts require a stage or space of their own regardless of the literary content. Substituting mythology and artificiality for experiential perspective, removes the ego of variation.

The following is a testament of pure lyrical and artful intensity. Characterized by extendibility, compassion, love and love lost; grounded courtesy of the balance in reality. Witness testimony inundated with stunning detail, rich allegories and timeless imagery:

~Ventricular Soliloquies~

To Be Continued…2012

Special Thanks

Telisha, Shana, Sonia, Yvelette, The Sabrees, Timothy Paule and all those who contributed to the successful publication of this book. Furthermore, much respect and appreciation to those who had a hand in making me the man that I am.

Mom, Dad, Christina, Leslie, Naim, Rhonda, Darren, Erika, Julius, Sister Clara Muhammad School Family—from way back (94 & Van Dyke), The Reeves, Vaughans, Robersons, Colvards, Moss, Dickersons, Van Irvins, Nelsons, Birds, Harrisons, Aunt Pat—The Caldwells, Khalifas, Bilal Smith family, Bilals, Mahdis, Rashads, Abdullahs, Mahmouds, Storys, Jordans, Porters, Davis, Coats, Lees, Wittens, Wileys, Ellisons, Gross, Browns, Lewis, Millers, Johnsons, Petites, Marks, Matthews, Garlands, Williams and the Buckners. Ron, Rico, Denise, Stanley, Sheldon, Zaire and a host of family/friends.

"It takes a village to raise a child"

~ African Proverb

Remembered Eternal

Grandma Nelson, Grandma Dickerson, Grandma Moss, Granddad Harrison, Granddad Moss, Granddad Dickerson, Godfather Reeves, Godfather Roberson, Godfather Wright, Godfather Vaughan, Aunt Donna, Aunt Marcia, Aunt Ruth, Uncle Wilber, Uncle Andrew, Uncle Jim, Uncle Robert, Uncle James, Charles (cousin), Mr. McFall, Mr. Smith, Mrs. Smith, Mr. Lee, Kevin Reynolds, Little John, Jackie, Omari (young cuz), Sterling Spears (Playboy), Dwayne Jordan, Lamarr Moy (Moe), Aaron Wynn (A-Juice), Robert Dunlap, Mychal Reeves, James Thorton, Ms. Thomas-Ponder, Mr. Nabors, Rasheedah Hanifa, Brother Ebby, Brother Michael, Brother Mahmoud, Brother Ali, Brother Tauheed, Sister Muhsinah, Hassan (S.C.M.S.), Sheldon Stegall (Meadowlane), DeAnna McCargo, J. Ellison, Mr. Ellison, Mrs. Ellison, Mr. Miller, Mrs. Stapleton, Charles Mitchell, WOO, Andre Graves, Trayvon Martin, Garland Johnson Jr. ('G') and all souljaz that I missed.

In the name of God I pray for: forgiveness of their faults, may their souls rest in peace, and that You grant them entrance into the kingdom of paradise to reside forever.

Amen.

The Only Way to Win

It takes a little courage
And a little self-control
And some grim determination,
If you want to reach the goal.
It takes a deal of striving,
And a firm and stern-set chin,
No matter what the battle,
If you really want to win.

There's no easy path to glory,
There's no rosy road to fame.
Life, however we may view it,
Is no simple parlor game;
But its prizes call for fighting,
For endurance and for grit;
For a rugged disposition
And a "don't-know-when-to-quit."

You must take a blow or give one,
You must risk and you must lose,
And expect that in the struggle
You will suffer from the bruise.
But you mustn't wince or falter,
If a fight you once begin;
Be a man and face the battle—-
That's the only way to win.

~Anonymous

www.ingramcontent.com/pod-product-compliance
Lightning Source LLC
Chambersburg PA
CBHW051950290426
44110CB00015B/2185